Wisdom of the Soul

Book 1

WISDOM OF THE SOUL: How to Live Life Created with Love and inSpiration Made Simple. Copyright © 2015 by Kerrie Wearing

All rights reserved. Printed in the Australia. No part of this book may be used or reproduced in any manner whatsoever without written permission except in the case of brief quotations embodied in critical articles or reviews.

Although the author and publisher have made every effort to ensure that the information in this book was correct at press time, the author and publisher do not assume and hereby disclaim any liability to any party for any loss, damage, or disruption caused by errors or omissions, whether such errors or omissions result from negligence, accident, or any other cause.

Some names and identifying details have been changed to protect the privacy of individuals.

Spirit Message by John Holland reprinted with permission

Book and Cover design by inSpirit Publishing
Editing by Nicolle Poll

ISBN: 978-0-9943028-0-9
First Edition: April 2015

For information contact;
inSpirit Publishing
28 Hickson Circuit, Harrington Park
Australian NSW 2567
www.inSpiritpublishing.net

Wisdom of the Soul

How to Live Life Created with Love & inSpiration made simple

Kerrie Wearing

Contents

Introduction	5
Part 1 - Journey to Oneness	16
A New Awareness	17
Living from Grace	34
Oneness	56
Recreation	70
Part 2 - Gifts of the Soul	94
Your Intuitive Self	95
Embracing the Ego	107
Naturally Psychic	125
Your Creative Spirit	141
Part 3 - Soul Centered Living	166
Career Choices	171
Aligning with Money	184
Soul Relationships	201

Contents Cont'd

Your Soul Purpose Revealed	214
Acknowledgements	221
About the Author	224

Dedication

For my children,
Nathan and Jessica.

Introduction

There is a shift happening within the consciousness of human kind. Yes, we all know of the existence of a higher power and consciousness we call God, Spirit, the Universe, Collective Consciousness or any term that is true and right for you, and many who understand this are living their truth within this awareness. Yet, there is even a more powerful shift happening within that understanding. People everywhere are really starting to take it to new levels beyond grasping the concept of living with this awareness and its effects on their lives. More and more people are opening themselves up to the realisation that Spirit is who we are, that we are the expression of God and the personification of the higher power and all we need do is live every moment of every day with the conscious awareness and knowing that this is true for all of us.

What this means, is that more and more people on this planet are living with the understanding of Oneness. Living with the knowing, we are all connected as One Divine Being and that how we live our lives has a direct influence on others and the evolution of the world and its future directions. More and more people are taking responsibility and being the change they want to see in this world.

When I say this, I'm not just talking about people understanding this from a logical perspective because that is what Spirituality is about. People are really getting it from the depths of their soul, they are living it in all aspects of their lives and who they are and this is great news. Because it means evolution is happening in the way the world needs it too. It can mean the difference between the human race surviving or not, between our planet continuing to supply life or not, to the end of war and world peace being achievable some time in the future. No, it may not occur in our lifetime or even in the next couple of generations, it is however now more than ever on track to manifesting. And you have a role to play in the creation of it, NOW! In reading this book, you are listening to your Soul speak, to it urges and if there is one thing I know about the Soul, it is that it knows it is centered in Oneness. Your Soul knows that you are connected to All that Is throughout all time and space, it knows you are here to contribute to humanity and raising awareness, it knows you are here to be love, to give love and it inspires you daily to live that truth whether you know this consciously now or not, is not important. What is important is that you listen, that you listen to the Soul urges that lead you forward, that you listen to your Soul speak and raise your own awareness in doing so. And you know what? I know you are listening and how do I know that. If you weren't listening, would you have picked up a book called Wisdom of the Soul? I don't think so. The fact that you are now reading this book speaks volumes about your listening within and that journey of Soul awareness you are living. So please, let me express my gratitude, not just for the opportunity you are giving me to share Wisdom of the Soul with you, but all for the difference you are making and contributing to the evolution of this world. From my Soul to yours, thank you.

My own personal shift into this new understanding began approximately three years ago. When I say this, I'm not talking about awakening my spirituality and living a life connected to Spirit, as that actually occurred nearly nineteen years ago. In fact, Spirit has been my life for all these years upon finding my passion and forging a career in helping people through the essence of Mediumship. What I am talking about here though, is the real existence of living and knowing you are Spirit in every moment of every day. Living with the total awareness that we are connected to everything and everyone in all time and space through the essence of Spirit. That, who we truly are, is centered in Oneness with this great universe and that in truth it hurts us to be anything else.

This shift for me began as I found myself questioning the spiritual belief that we are here on this earth to learn lessons. This belief is a train of thought that a lot of spiritually aware people hold, especially those in psychic, mediumship and Spiritualist circles. Yet for me, I finally came to the realization that while it can provide purpose and understanding to every challenge and experience you have which then gives you a sense of peace. It can also have you in a constant state of struggle as you strive to look for meaning and the lesson in every life experience, especially those when life isn't going so well. This for me, after sixteen years had me on my knees feeling spent, soul weary and saying to the Universe *"enough is enough"*. However, once I let go of this belief and came to understand it was all about my choices, that I could learn to grow and evolve from JOY and a place of Peace, or the daily grind of struggle and continually looking within for the lesson, my inner world began to change dramatically. This change in belief perpetuated a whole new journey of self discovery which unfolded a different perspective on Spirit, on life, on the spiritual values I hold and even on my approach to Mediumship and my work.

Wisdom of the Soul: How to Live Life Created with Love and Inspiration Made Simple is a unique approach to living your daily life from knowing your soul intimately, and living a life that expresses this in the deepest and most purposeful ways. The fullest expression of my soul in my sense of Oneness with this Universe lies in writing and teaching. This book brings both of these elements of my soul together, in a way that I believe will serve you and transform your life, just as this new information has transformed mine.

Of course, it is necessary to begin with some basics. Yet, in visiting these basics, you will find new perspectives and new understandings as you look deeper into what is this thing we call our Soul? How does it relate to your everyday life and the spiritual expression of your life. How does it connect you to the Divine? And how can you epitomise who we are spiritually while living the human experience?

These are just some of the questions being answered throughout Wisdom of the Soul. My intention is to provide you with access to the wisdom and tools, which will enable you to have a conversation with your soul each and everyday. In doing so, you'll find that your life will take on a whole new look. One with more meaning, more purpose, more love and more inSpiration.

You will find that peace, JOY and happiness become your friend while you become a master at steering yourself gracefully through life's challenges. From experience you will recognize and know that your answers lie within and it is only a matter of seeking them out with ease and grace.

Success will be something that comes to you easily in all of its forms as your need to assist others has you rejoicing in giving back and being of service in ways that reflect who you are and what is important to you.

If you have ever heard the expression *"We are spiritual beings having a human experience." Wisdom of the Soul* will guide you to know the true meaning of this phrase. To know and experience yourself as a spiritual being. To live your life from the heart and soul of who you truly are, the Light of Spirit and a Divine Being of Love. This book will help you to make it real so it is not just a phrase that gets bandied without any real thought for what the essence of the phrase truly means.

I promise you, that the information contained within the following pages will have you knowing you are the Light of Spirit while providing the inSpiration and the techniques to keep it real on a daily basis. I will share with you the daily tools that work for me and for the many others I have shared them with, to stay in tune with your soul, to listen and inSpire you to take action where it is needed. To heed the call of your Soul and its purpose while working towards creating a life that not only expresses this, but also gives you the freedom to enjoy the life you deserve to live.

We can't do this without covering the everyday important topics of relationships, career, and money, so we will discuss these in depth as well with the intention of empowering you in each of these areas, as I'm sure they are important to you. We will highlight the creative being you are, enriching your life as recognise the power of your Creative Spirit and we will also spend time expanding your awareness of communicating in new ways. Communicating from within, Spirit to Spirit as we explore how knowing you are the Light of Spirit unfold the gifts of your Soul with psychic awareness, intuition and mediumship.

It is important for me to mention how I apply some terms and the words I use throughout Wisdom of the Soul for ease and clarity for you. For me the word God and the word the Divine, represent the same source, the energy and source that we call come from, the higher consciousness and power and the source of this great universe. Please use or substitute whichever label that works and resonates for you that means the same source, Collective Consciousness, Great Spirit, All That Is, the choice is yours and what is true for you.

I use the terms Spirit, the Divine Spirit within and the Spark of the Divine to represent that part of you that is connected to God, the Divine and All That Is.

The word Ego is used largely to describe that part of you that can operate in fear, doubt and works towards keeping you disconnected and separate, though I do personally recognise the Ego as also being that part of you that identifies you as you, including all of your glorious positive human attributes though for clarity and descriptive purposes, I've used the word Self to describe this combination of who we are and lastly, the word Soul and Soul self is used and attributed to who we are when whole, complete and in Oneness which incorporates the completeness of our Spirit, , self and our connections to All That Is.

Where once you saw a glimmer of who you truly are, *Wisdom of the Soul: How to Live Life Created with Love and Inspiration Made Simple* will help you to expand and open this up beyond your expectations to an even greater awareness of your Soul, the creative being you are and how living with this knowing in each moment is not only infinitely rewarding, it is much simpler to do than you may realise.

Part One

Journey to Oneness

A New Awareness

When I first became aware of myself as a spiritual being, of universal energy and that the existence of a higher consciousness had value and meaning in my life after my brother Allen took his own life in 1995, I was filled with excitement, enthusiasm and was so in awe of the new world around me, I couldn't get enough information to satisfy my thirst for knowledge. This time of awakening in your life is such a special and valuable time when the universe is opening up to you in similar ways, that I hope you are experiencing similar levels of passion and enthusiasm. These days, I feel such joy for people I meet who are at this crossroads in their life, I am excited for them and grateful to them for it inSpires me with my own memories and the feeling of excitement of that time in my life. Each and every little external sign I received and acknowledged had huge meaning. Every occurance of synchronicity had me in awe of this great universe. As it still does.

This new phase of awareness usually does begin with learning to read how the universe speaks to you. The butterfly visits, the feather drops, the chance meetings and the 'co-incidences' all take on new meaning so effortlessly and often with an unbridled passion. Nothing goes unnoticed as a sign from Spirit and the very existence of the synchronistic events which lead you forward are validation that your heart is open and connected to the Universe. At this time in my journey, I had wonderful assistance from Denise Linn with her book Signposts: The Universe is Whispering to you. This book became my companion throughout this time and has remained a staple of the books I recommend to others for when you are seeking to expand your knowledge of signs and symbols. Before long your awareness will deepen as you begin to understand that there is more to life than you at first perceive and you open your mind to the belief that you are a Soul with a body. One, where the Soul comprises of the Self which is often readily referred to as the Ego, along with a connection to Divinity which I refer to as your Divine Spirit. It is this Divine connection we aim to give more of voice each day. In the centered world we have been born and raised in, most of us usually come to awaken our spirituality having had the being the dominant force within. It is now time to bring about a balance between your Divine Spirit and the Ego so there is a greater sense of peace and harmony with a daily awareness of how the Divine weaves it's connectedness throughout all of your life. While this process takes many years, in so doing you know this balance naturally takes care of the human triumvirate of the mind, body and soul and you can begin to see yourself as a Soul connected to all things and all beings throughout all of time and space. Living with this awareness and more importantly this Knowing, will have you experience yourself and your life in Oneness, connected to All That Is.

As you begin expanding your awareness to lay a strong foundation with living from the Soul, it is necessary to firstly gain an understanding of the Soul, the Spirit, their purpose and how they work together to provide a unique human experience.

Your Soul is the vehicle through which the body travels, meaning your Soul houses the body, not the other way around where your body has a soul. Being energetic by nature allows the Soul to be omnipresent, easily transformed and intuitively connected to All That Is. It is also the vehicle through which your Spirit, your Divine connection expressions itself. Imagine the Soul being the middle man, integrating the body and all of your humanness with that of Spirit and All That Is.

The Soul has the capacity to seek harmony as it aligns with the energy of the Divine or equally it can remain separated with a continual need to individualise and empower the Self. Neither of these components of the Soul are separate entities, they are a part of the whole Soul Self yet we seek to separate and right now for the purpose congruence and with the current level of human understanding of the Soul, it helps to label them separately. So we call them, the Divine Spirit within, the Ego or the Self when in actuality they are all the Soul Self.

For many years I have believed that the human energetic field we know as the Aura, is actually the Soul. I still know this to be true with one big difference. The Aura in all of its glorious beauty is often perceived for its physical characteristics, such as the energetic layers, it's emotional and energetic responsibilities and its highlights of colour. All of which, I have written about in depth in my first book *A New Kind of Normal: Unlock the Medium Within*. Investing in some study on the intricacies of the Aura will certainly increase your soul awareness and I do recommend you take some time to do this, however in placing too much emphasis on the composition of the Aura you can often overlook its true purpose, which is to integrate our Divine Spirit into the here and now with the human experience.

When you begin awaking the connection between Soul and Spirit by aligning the Soul with Divinity, it is your soul, which helps you to find purpose and meaning in all of your life experiences. It is through your Soul that you make sense of all the ups and downs in life. It is through the Soul, rightly or wrongly that we create our lives as we know them. It carries within it all that you are. Your life experiences good and bad, your hearts desires, your relationship connections and past life knowings through out all time and space, your self and your divine self as it is in human form all exist within the Soul. Importantly, it also maintains a connection to what people commonly call the Akashic Records, a universal database recording all that can be known about yourself throughout all time and space. As I know and understand it, this information is not recorded out in some universal ether, it is more intimately housed within your Soul Self allowing you access to it, should you have enough detachment and can be objective enough to receive the information with clarity and to not be too overwhelmed by it all. Knowing all this lies within gives you ownership, personal responsibility and therefore a power over who you choose to be and the life you choose to live.

When we die, all energy has the capacity to change form, which incidently we are constantly doing here in life as well. Aligning with the Divine has you in a constant state of renewal and rebirth, aiming to be the fullest expression of who your Soul Self truly is. This essentially is what occurs naturally at the moment our Soul transitions from this world. No boundaries exist to restrict who you are, no fear of judgment, no fear of being hurt only the freedom to be who you truly are for you know nothing but love. And yet, this is exactly the journey your Divine Spirit is guiding you on now, to know all of this while in human form. I don't know about you, why would you wait until you die to know this, when you can know the fullest expression of your Divine Soul Self now.

"There is no greater a powerful being than the Soul that is consciously connected to all that they are, all that they can be while fully realising that in their life."

I love that last sentence as I felt its essence and power flow through me while writing it for you. This is the Wisdom of the Soul and to unfold this in your life it is important to make self awareness a daily discipline. The power of self awareness is the foreground to self actualising all that you want and the being that you are. Living with the daily awareness of the Soul and aligning your Soul to Divinity, first and foremost before all else everyday, allows the essence of Spirit to flow through all that you are, all that you are connected to and therefore all that life is for you. Including those you love, your home, your work and all that you hold near and dear to you.

Let's begin the new journey of awareness by aligning yourself with the principal that you can learn to grow and evolve through the experience of JOY as opposed to pain and struggle. As I mentioned in the introduction, there is a commonly held belief that life is our classroom and to grow and evolve we do so by the learning of lessons. In my experience, this certainly did help me to grow and evolve however, along with that I also created a life of constant struggle as I continually looked for the lesson in all of life's experiences. One after the other, they would come along for years on end. Then I came to choose a different belief, that life is our playground for us to experience all that we are, through all that we do. A belief that allows me to grow and evolve with JOY, life really began to change.

Specifically, for the last five nearly six years, my focus had been on wanting to change my thoughts, beliefs and experience around abundance and in particular money. Initially the old way of being had me changing my mindset, uncovering my emotional blocks and releasing any baggage I had concerning all of these, which I am grateful for. During those years I personally had changed within and felt very different about money and abundance in my life and I certainly grew into a natural attitude of gratitude. No longer was it a kick in the guts whenever I needed to rob Peter to pay Paul. However, I was still robbing Peter to pay Paul. Externally, life hadn't changed and that was the aim.

It finally started to dawn on me that in the constant looking within, I was always going to find something to change or that needed to be 'fixed'. Although now I could see these were really no longer getting in the way of achieving what I wanted to. What had been getting in the way all along was how I see myself. I needed to stop seeing myself as something that needed to be fixed and see myself as the whole and complete spiritual being I am, reflected in the image of the Divine Light of Love.

This is what I offer you here with the teachings contained within Wisdom of the Soul. To see yourself, not as someone who needs to be 'fixed', or someone who is in the 'darkness' needing to let more light and love in. What I offer you here will have you knowing not only are you the Divine Spirit, but a whole and complete spiritual being born in the likeness of God, with the power to choose a life of purpose, joy and contentment.

Personally, my favourite tool to use to communicate within daily is what I call the Soul Conversation. They are easy, so simple and yet highly effective to empower you with intuition, insight and understanding. Communicating with our Soul Self should be a natural process that easily works integrates into your daily life helping you to keep your soul awareness high and at the optimum. My daily Soul Conversation questions are an effective and intuitive way to do this. Directing a simple soul conversation question within always yields an answer that with consistency, allows that voice to grow stronger.

At first should you find it a challenge, pre-empt the question with a few deep breaths and place your hand over your heart to assist in centering your awareness. Then relax and allow the answer to flow forward into your mind. Accept the first thought, feeling or even imagery that presents and try not eradicate it with doubt. Accept with love and you will find each day a delightful surprise. Here is your first Soul Conversation.

Exercises

Using your journal, answer this Soul Conversation question and use the following meditation to identify how you see and experience you and your life right now. How well do you see your Spirit weaving itself throughout your life?

In my life JOY comes to me in the following ways:

Meditation - Calling You Home:

This visualisation I call *Calling You Home*, is designed to gather your soul by calling back your energy and all the pieces of your Soul, which are energetically entwined with people, places and circumstances that do not serve you. This could be causing physical and emotional disturbances within your soul, or at the very least detracting from your sense of peace. Aiming for a sense of wholeness, this exercise will lay some of the groundwork to begin your journey to Oneness.

Before you begin, take some time to set the mood so it is in tune with your soul. Perhaps some soft music and lighting will help to create a gentle, welcoming energy. I suggest also having your journal and favourite chair ready and inviting.

As you take your seat, I want you to know you are free from distractions for at least the next ten minutes. Settle into a nice rhythm of breathing deeply in through the nose and out through the mouth. As you do this a few times, you will feel yourself settle into that space within that speaks of peace and harmony. Focus your awareness here, allowing no distractions. Keep breathing and….

- Imagine yourself in a field on a beautiful summers day. In this field you feel the warmth of the sun's rays and are becoming mindful of all that nature is offering, around you. You notice the field of wildflowers and any animals that may also be residents of your field.

- As you look around, to the left you notice a small, gentle waterfall with a very inviting pool of water. So inviting in fact, you can't wait to immerse yourself and feel the water all over you.

- So you hurry along and before you know it, you are standing right in the depths of this glorious waterfall. Showering yourself with all that it has to offer.

- Immediately you begin to feel like your true self as the water washes away all your worries, cares and anything troubling your mind. With this you really start to relax and you notice your breathing start to slow.

- Standing beneath this waterfall, you feel a growing presence of strength and centeredness while your connection to the Divine is becoming all encompassing. In this moment your sense of power is growing. Yet there is more.

- In this moment you slowly start to become aware that there are parts of your energy entwined throughout your universe that may not be beneficial, serving you well or even quite distinctly detracting from the wholeness of your Spirit & Soul.

- As the knowingness of each instance arrives into your awareness, speak mindfully to your soul requesting its return home with these words.

"Divine Spirit of me, I love you and care for you so deeply, that I no longer wish for you to engage in energies be it people, places or circumstances that do not lift us up and hold our being in love and joy. Please come back to me in Wholeness and Harmony."

- Do this for each instance that arises. As you feel this come to its completion, please take some more time to continue cleansing beneath your waterfall and embrace all that you are with love.

- When you feel the time is right, allow the imagery to dissipate and return your awareness to the room you are in and your body. In your own time, opening your eyes.

Time now to journal, have a cuppa and enJOY the Wisdom of your Soul.

Living from Grace

When you live a life inspired by your Soul, you will find your will is strong to find within yourself that very place that is your connection to God, your connection to Source, the Higher Consciousness or whatever term may be right for you.

It is here, that your God consciousness begins by being that little voice inside you, keeping you on track to align with Divinity and unveil your Soul purpose, guiding you and making itself known often when you are at your most vulnerable. This part of your Soul, I call your Spirit is rooted in the nature of the Divine and expresses itself through your Higher Self.

You can equate your Higher Self to a being within you that is totally and complicitly aware that you are a spiritual being living a very human experience. Your Higher Self is the go between your higher spiritual consciousness and your human conscious awareness, with a language that begins with mild, if somewhat unrecognized intuition through to a direct link of open communication spoken through intuition, emotion and clairaudience. Clairaudience being your psychic ability to hear audibly within the mind, the guidance and instructions from your higher self just as you would receive a mediumship communication from a loved one in Spirit in the same way. It is all Spirit to Spirit communication.

A workable connection to your Higher Self such as this can be a very powerful attribute when living from the Soul. You'll find your emotions playing a key role in indicating how well you are living from your soul and increasing how much influence your Spirit can contribute. As you come to know your emotional self more intimately, you will learn to identify quite easily when you are in your Soul space and not in your head. This is quite simply achieved by being aware of your emotions each day and moment to moment.

When you live from the Soul with a focus of giving your Divine Spirit a greater say in who you are and therefore your life, there are real tangible effects and benefits that you feel and see in doing this, and they begin with the Seven Soul States of Grace.

While my interpretations vary based on personal inspiration from Spirit, you may also recognize these from the Bible verse Galatians 5: 22 where they are commonly known as the Fruits of the Spirit.

Personally I have come to know each one and can identify life lessons and learning around each of them as I allowed that aspect of Spirit to become a natural part of who I am. In an effort to assist you with coming to know each Soul State of Grace as I have, I have included an affirmation with each one. Affirmations enable you to raise your awareness of the contents of your mind, your emotions and are a powerful tool to increasing your sense of self awareness. There are three key factors to achieving success when working with affirmations and I offer you those here with the intent they help you to work more fluently with affirmations.

- Write your affirmation in the vain of having already achieved your goal, with a sense of gratitude and appreciation. This works towards using the energy to create the reality, while also instilling gratitude, which is a strong magnet for success.

- It is important when creating and reciting your affirmation to generate the feeling along with it. How will the experience feel when you have achieved what it is you are affirming?

- Writing out the affirmation and displaying it somewhere you can see it often throughout the day such as on the bathroom mirror when brushing your teeth or visiting for a tinkle is not only productive but much easier than having to try to remember it throughout the day, giving you a greater potential to stay with it.

Soul State of Awareness

I'm beginning with Awareness for two reasons, firstly as I mentioned previously Awareness is the precursor to the changes life brings when you live a Soul inSpired life. It is the very fabric of being aware that brings about the following six Soul States of Grace and not just as one off occurances now and then but as sustained states of being. They all become who you are, enabling you to live a life that flows with ease and grace. While there will still be upheavals and times when you are challenged by life circumstances, it is through awareness and its gift of purpose and meaning that even in the face of adversity you can still manage to find a sense of peace and an understanding as to why life is being so ungracious.

Affirmation: *I am really enjoying being totally aware of all I need to today, thank you.*

Soul State of Humility

It is a natural state for a soul that is totally aware of itself to be present in a state of humbleness.

The usual order of living in current societies of western culture has us growing up in a way that validates and nurtures our and its need for separation. By , in this instance I mean the aspect of your Soul self that seeks to identify itself as an individual which strives to keep us in separation from All That Is and usually does so through a never ending struggle of doubt, fear, seeking approval and essentially trying to overcome any pain we ever experienced by not being loved in the way we need to be. Understand that after years of living from the self where a western upbringing largely nurtures that part of us that is full of doubt. It is time to give rise to the Divinity within and align more purposefully with the aspect of the soul that loves, nurtures and inspires.

In my personal experience, this initial process of humbling and balance took twelve long years, I like most people had minimal awareness and understanding of spirituality. I can even remember receiving a psychic reading and being told in six months I would become spiritual. At the time, I had no concept of what the word meant. I actually needed to learn that I had a Soul, which is comprised of my Spirit and my as I understood at the time.

It wasn't until the end of the twelve year journey that I could see and know of the tug of war within myself between the Spirit and the Ego, when that internal struggle finally ceased to exist for me. This occurred on my very first trip to Sedona Arizona, where the coming together of many years of self healing, a significant past life connection and the energy of the land and my connection to it brought about a moment of healing and coupled with a feeling of having come home, like I had not felt before or since.

This healing eradicated the internal struggle as my finally came to know its place and I came to know and appreciate myself as a much more humble and intuitive being. This resulted in my being more capable of a heightened awareness as to when my was getting in the way and therefore allowing me to make even more empowered choices while acting with greater humility in a lot of ways.

This process of humbling one's is a natural process, which will take many years. We all begin our lives from a state of egoic coercion where your life and behaviours play to the needs of , continually validating its need for separation and individualization protecting you from perceived harm based on prior experience. It is from this state that we begin our spiritual awakening and begin to give your Divine Spirit within a greater voice. The needs to make room and having years of being in control, often its hold is strong and it tends to never want to relax or quiet down easily, even putting up a strong fight in some cases which is where you really need to be careful, for if you do not keep your self awareness high by learning to be completely open and honest with yourself you will fail to recognise when the is at play. It will continue to trick you, even claiming to be your Spirit only to win the battle and you will become stuck here at this point of personal growth and soul's evolution. Never reaching the heights of JOY that can be experienced.

Sadly, some of those at the greatest risk of this occurring can be those who practice in the psychic arts. I've seen it all too often where psychics and mediums are very good at focusing all their attention on serving others, enhancing their psychic abilities yet never fully realizing the importance of serving the self first and placing as much importance on self awareness as they do on how great that reading was, or where is my next opportunity to reach more people.

I'm not saying all psychics and mediums are of this nature, as there are many who are not and you will find these are the ones who have spent a lot of time, in training and development continually seeking to know themselves to greater depths before they venture forth to use their abilities to help others.

Humbleness is a natural gift of the Soul that is aligned with Divinity and one that once achieved becomes a natural behaviour that needs no thinking or forethought, for it is a natural state of being.

Affirmation: *To be humble is not to know that you are, yet I truly appreciate acting with humbleness in all that I do today. Thank you.*

Soul State of Servitude

Servitude, like humility is another natural gift of the Soul when in alignment with the Divine Spirit. At the heart of all Spirit is the need to do for another, to treat others in ways that bring love into this world. Your connection to the Divine has the innate knowing that this is what the world needs, more servitude and humanity towards others.

This can and will be expressed through a variety of ways though it will underlie everything you do. Some of you may even find that your Soul's true purpose is intricately connected with being of service to others, as is mine. My soul's evolutionary intended purpose for this incarnation is to evolve through being of service to others and I know this is inexplicably linked with a past life where I wasn't so humble or giving, even taking the lives for others for my own monetary gain. Not something I relish being a part of!

When being of service in the true sense of the word, you will find your only intention, your only thoughts are to assist and make a difference for those who are receiving from you. There is no expectation of receiving in return and there is a JOY and a wisdom that comes from being of service when it is from a deeper part of your soul.

Your soul rises to the occasion and the only gratification you need is how it feels to give to another in this way. The challenge is to let go of your own needs and wants, enough to allow the Divine Spirit within to flow. This creates a sense of magnitude which equates to all parties, including you having their needs met in the deepest of ways naturally. This is in itself is a very humbling experience as you feel the presence of this Spirit to Spirit connection and know that your Divine purpose in coming together is being served.

Affirmation: *In mastering the art of Servitude, I offer myself in Divine Service today. Please use me as your humble servant to do good and gracious deeds for all concerned. Thank you.*

Soul State of Acceptance

Literally, one of the most challenging Soul states to achieve, but well worth the hard work and effort in coming to understand and appreciate what being in the state of full Acceptance has install for you.

Acceptance belies a state of frustration, so when you feel a sense of frustration it really indicates that your soul is resisting where it needs to be right now. Life often has a way of taking control all by itself and no matter how much you try to effect change by working with your inner being or by taking action, sometimes you are meant to be exactly where you are with all that life entails. This is especially true when your Spiritual Destiny is influencing you in a big way and you have yet to fully comprehend what that means and involves.

So when you are feeling frustrated, delve a little deeper into the cause of this frustration by being open and honest with yourself and you will find that your ability to surrender where things are at, a whole lot easier. As they say *"Let go and Let God"*.

Otherwise, with ongoing resistance the only other outcome is you reaching the inevitable tipping point, the emotional crisis point, which will have you on your knees surrendering and feeling emotionally spent. Should this be how Acceptance unfolds for you as it did me, the key here is to not give up on all that you want. To accept what is for now while maintaining all you are working towards.

Affirmation: *I accept all that I am, all that I can be and all that my life is. I let go of what I* *do not know or understand and trust that you, Divine Spirit will lead me forward.*

Soul State of Peace

As I begin writing these paragraphs on Peace, my higher self would like to start this section with some channeling.

"My humble servant, Peace comes from within, while being achieved through the act of Mindfulness which is a choice you make, every moment of everyday. It is very possible for one to be at the center of a storm, yet within there be a calmness and sense of serenity. This is a disciplined nature achieved through very powerful mindfulness techniques which work towards raising your awareness of your truth, your thoughts and your emotional well being. It is in this space you then have the power to choose whether what is occurring within, is to be let go, to change the repetitive pattern or to hold on. There is just one important point to remember here – Letting go creates peace.

And now I return to you to your author, Thank you"

Elaborating on this, holding on and trying to control the outcomes of life creates a structure and security, yet it yields turmoil when life inevitably threatens your structure and therefore your sense of security around it. This happens daily from small, passive, insignificant ways which largely go unnoticed, yet can have your over reacting through to ways you realise consciously, do affect you such as burying a loved one.

Letting go creates an energy of fluidity that enables you to flow with the roller coaster of life, one day at a time being in the Now and embracing all that is with you in the moment. This creates a sense of peace as you know all you have is the Now. But more importantly, you also know that all you need is with you in that Now.

Affirmation: *Peace is at the heart of who I am today, and I am grateful for the understanding and knowledge that takes me away from that. Thank you.*

Soul State of Love

Love is the personification of the Divine. In our hearts we feel the presence of God, through the power of love. It is this spark of light that when revealed to you, allows you to know yourself in the reflection of others, through the love of your children, the love of nature, the love of others and the love of all that is. When you know yourself in this way, you will know yourself as the true spiritual being you are reflected as an expression of the Divine and its powerful source of love.

We know the most powerful manifestation of the Divine's light of love occurs on the day you are born. We feel it evolve from nothingness into love that can be felt between a new born baby and its parents. In that moment, no matter the circumstances surrounding the birth, the presence of God can be felt. Knowing this is the infant, the Divine being of love and pure innocence. Yet, as the child grows and evolves into adulthood, this life and all it entails works unconcsiously to dimish this love and work towards keeping you separate from the Divine. This pure unconditional feeling of love is then often replaced with a love that is reflected and limited in being accepted. We grow to know we are loved if we feel accepted for who we are and what we do. This occurs in all levels of society, from in the home to the more broader reaching avenues such as celebritism and even religion. This is how we are conditioned from birth, passed on from generation to generation leaving us devoid of knowing the true power of love. This unconscious conditioning becomes all that you know and therefore can feel 'right' because it is generational and societal. Yet you have the ability to live with awareness, change this cycle and gift a new understanding to the future generations so they too can go on and experience love in new ways.

Make a choice today to bring yourself back to knowing love is the Divine working in your life. Doing this is not as difficult as you may think. Wading through the murky waters of your Soul can be a joyful experience if you choose it and begin by checking in with yourself, daily. Empower your soul by giving it the time and dedication it deserves. Don't get so caught up in the doing and living from a to do list that any hope of honouring the little urging from your Soul can go too easily unnoticed.

One of my clients Christine had recently lost her mum, and moved home to New Zealand to take on a greater responsibility with the family. While knowing in her heart this was where she was meant to be, she was also feeling devoid of any guidance and feeling unsupported by Spirit and the Universe. This was leaving her to question her faith and her spiritual connection while wandering what was the point of it all. No answers, nor any snippets of help and guidance were forthcoming, leaving Christine struggling to break this cycle. During our consultation, for me there was really only one piece of intuitive guidance that Christine needed, and that was to listen and honour her Soul urgings. In real terms, this meant the next time she felt an urge to go and meditate, to sit in solitude with nature, to heal, to dance or to say no, Christine needed to do it! Not wait until she's cooked dinner, done the grocery shopping, taken the kids here or there. Christine needed to make a conscious choice to put herself first more often. We get so caught up in "oh I will, but I need to do this first" that what usually occurs next is that you never get around to connecting with your Soul, because life has gotten in the way. Then before too long the cycle keeps repeating itself and your Soul eventually goes quiet giving up and receding into ill health, all the while you are left mentally asking for help and for guidance from Spirit.

In taking action and listening to the inner urgings of her Soul, Christine's guidance would make itself known, leading her to where she needs to be, to what she needs to do and to heal as she needs to, all the while allowing for life's obligations which are always treated with respect and factored into anything that may be of importance to your Soul. Loving yourself first in this way does not mean being selfish. Far from it. You are in essence giving to yourself so you can then continue to give to others. To be the best you can be for others, and showing the important people in your life that you matter, and more importantly teaching them to love themselves too.

While making a change of this nature can be hard to do for some people, it is just a matter of making a mindset change. Being mindful to incorporate some form of self love in your day, every day and allowing yourself to honour your Soul's urges will naturally result in life taking on a greater flow of ease and grace. The balance you may be looking for will come, and you will soon be looking back wondering what you did to have balance and love show up in your life.

Affirmation: Love is all that I am and all that I am being.

Soul State of Joy

JOY is a vibration we experience when our mind and our heart is in alignment with our Soul. It is the very real feeling of exhuberation and love, when all levels of who we are in that moment comes together in full connection and appreciation with Divinity.

We come to know this experience of JOY by moving emotionally and spiritually through each of the other six Soul states of Grace. It is in knowing them and having them present in your life that JOY becomes a part of who you are. JOY is a natural part of the soul, just as breathing is to each of us. There is no spiritual work needed which can equate to JOY, simply allow it in by focusing your intention on living from your Spirit and these previous Soul States of Grace I have described.

JOY is the reward.

Oneness

"Oneness - when the heart knows no boundaries and as a result we feel compelled to do nothing but live who we truly are, living to the Soul's fullest expression of itself."

Oneness is a state of being whereby the very fabric of your Divine Spirit is woven through the energy of all people and all things. The very nature of understanding this brings about an awareness of living this in truth, which will then lead you to a path of experiencing Oneness as your conscious reality.

How does Oneness look and feel in your life?

You feel the heartbeat of all life. Your intuition springs forth naturally as you sense, feel, know and intuit things about others, which are usually beyond the veil of perception.

Your everyday thoughts along with your intuitive thoughts become one. You experience thought provoked by intuition and knowingness are no longer distinguishably separate or discernable from your everyday thoughts. Nor do they need to be.

All of life has a flow and graciousness to it. Where once, you may have encountered coming up against brick walls, hotspots and counter productive energy, you now flow with the river of life. This shows itself with your life taking on a natural pace of all its own, as opposed to the fast pace of modern society. From the ease of parking spots appearing, to less disruption and disagreements being more easily diffused your life now effuses more harmony.

Your ability to access and understand yourself to even greater spiritual depths is increased as you now have the capacity to know and understand all that is relevant to defining this incarnation, including your soul purpose and the life circumstances which are designed to support that journey.

Coming to know Oneness for me was a gradual progression of my spiritual growth and understanding, until a multitude of events occurred all at once culminating in the actualization of Oneness and its relevance to my life and my sense of self.

At the time a colleague of mine was experimenting with a new healing modality, which incorporates kinesiology and she was looking for people to trial this with to grow her understanding. As I lay on the healing bed and opened myself up to the experience, I could feel my heart chakra (energy centre) stirring. It had been quite a while since I lay on a healing bed and without my usual healing practitioner, I was keen to see what would unfold.

This healing modality called for me to request an area of life I would like to work on and receive healing for. I asked for this focus to be on my finances which was area I had struggled with for a few years leading up to that point. As I lay on the bed and my colleague began using the muscle testing of Kinesiology to determine where my emotional block concerning this issue lied and at what age it began, I couldn't help but think that this process was not allowing for someone who has a strong sense of self awareness or who had carried out a lot of self healing over the years. So when my colleague struggled to hit on an emotional occurance that resonated with me, I later realised the relevance of my thoughts.

This healing left me feeling out of sorts for days. The only way I can describe how I felt was that my soul felt 'dirty', like it had been touched in places it didn't need to be. I believe the Soul is always going to maintain an imprint and memory of everything that you experience over time, yet with healing our aim is to diminish and heal the emotional attachment associated with the experience and the affect it still may have on your life.

This form of healing combined with a lack of intuition from the practitioner, did not cater for the amount of healing that had already occurred. It targeted the imprint whether there was still emotional attachment or not. This left me feeling unsettled for days with a little frustration building as well. Frustration due to the fact, that my colleague had many years of professional experience and my expectations of being treated and supported through what was to follow as a result were not met. My efforts to offer how I felt with honesty, to offer my professional opinion on the consultation (which was being asked for as part of the trial) were being rejected by my colleague and instead I was told that it was all fear I was holding onto and resisting, which was later recountered by the practitioner.

As usually is the case, the gift in this experience came in the days following as I was processing the detrimental energetic effects that had occurred. I had been left completely drained of energy and it felt like my heart chakra had been tapped into and was now a constant flow of releasing energy just like a tap of running water. Only I was not filling up again. I was struggling to function and was certainly not refuelling with energy. In amidst all of this, I felt that during the healing I had opened up enough to take on energy from the environment and from my colleagues other healing clients even though she assured me of her strict cleansing rituals.

I felt my heart chakra had opened and released while being connected to the Universe, though I was confused as to why the outcome resulted in this non stop draining of energy. I knew enough to know that this was not at all how connecting as One to the Universe and All That Is should feel. It should be a powerful omnipotent feeling, full of JOY, love and a feeling that is so addictive you can't get enough of it.

Eventually after day five of the constant drain of energy, it finally dawned on me to ask Spirit for guidance. I can be a bit slow on the up take at times! I simple asked "If my heart has opened up enough to allow a connection to everything as One, why was the response this drain of energy I feel?"

Here was the response from Spirit as I sat down to journal the next day. "From the moment of conception, your existence came about stressfully, all felt through the womb. Into life you came and the day to day battle for survival was also felt along with the neediness of others. You saw your place in this world to give love and you still do. Never having it returned through expression, left an empty well where giving and receiving is concerned. To the glorious little blonde haired girl (my inner child) - don't change sweetheart, give all you have to give, just be sure to give as much love to yourself as you would to others. For if you get that right, then there is balance and you do not need it from others if they can not give it to you in the way you expect or better yet. You'll feel it and accept it from them in the ways they only know how to give it. Acceptance."

At this point the drain of energy began to rectify itself and I began to experience a new way of being. In understanding all of this about myself and taking real day to day action to love myself and experience it through all that I do, my sense of connection to others has multiplied ten fold. My sense of JOY is limitless as I find my heart bursting with excitement and joy for life beyond what I felt before. This is how Oneness should feel, and I am so grateful for its presence in my life.

This experience defined the meaning of Oneness for me. Being in Oneness with All That Is occurs when the heart knows no boundaries to love and as a result we feel compelled to do nothing but live who we truly are, living to the Soul's fullest expression of itself.

Who you Truly are in Oneness.

One of my greatest wishes is for you to know who you truly are when living in Oneness. Knowing this gives you the power to choose who you are in every moment in every day. Are you the light we all know you to be? Are you the true spiritual being you were born to be? Bringing your uniqueness to this world, loving others, riding the storms with grace, filling any void you have with action to heal and change. Do you see yourself as special, a bright light, the heart and soul of your life? Bringing with it all, JOY and a mesmerising energy for everyone you come in contact with.

Or do you see yourself in darkness, where life and you are complex, constantly in a struggle to lift yourself out of the difficulties you face. Seeing yourself less than who you truly are, worried about the opinions and expectations of others, a head often full of negative self talk and doubt, and constantly in the hunt to "get somewhere".

Old and more traditional views of spirituality tell us that we are light and we need to embrace it or let it in. This implies the light is out there somewhere, or we need to break down the darkness by changing who we are constantly to reveal who we truly are. For me, having travelled this road for a many years, I know it all equates to engaging in a constant struggle. Yes, self healing is important and my next book, Wisdom of the Soul: The Healer Within is going to cover this topic in greater depth, yet can I share with you a little secret. The process of self healing does not need to be as difficult or challenging as we tend to make it. Healing can be brought about through the experience of JOY as you see yourself reflected in the light, as opposed to the darkness.

Where once we would focus our thoughts, attention and healing on the negative aspects of ourselves, delving deep into why we came to be this way and what occurred in our life to have us respond or behave in certain ways as a consequence. What hurts remain buried to stop us being who we want to be, or stop us achieving what we want to achieve.

Going forward, it is more relevant to embrace who you are amongst all of this. Free yourself from the limitations these hurts offer by choosing to know yourself in Oneness. In Oneness, you are the all knowing being created in the likeness of God. In Oneness you know and understand the purpose to these experiences and are free to let go of any negative emotional attachment to the experience you are maintaining that may be holding you back.

In living this energy and awareness of Oneness, I already am who I am aiming to be, I already am ALL THAT I AM and all I need do is choose to be it. You see at the moment of creation when the aspects of your soul came to be, to enrich this life's experience you were created whole. All of you, the self that is loving, all knowing and the spiritual being you are as well as the self that is devoid of love, resides in and lacks self love. The Ying and the Yang of you already exists. You only need choose which side of yourself do you give more power to.

Therefore with this exercise, I'd love to gift you with the power to choose and know yourself in Oneness, so you can live with the knowing you truly are a loving, unique and powerful spiritual being.

To do so, I have the Ultimate Soul Conversation for you, one question to answer but before you do that please clear and prepare the space you will work in. Set the mood so it is in tune with your soul. Soft music and lighting, create a gentle, welcoming energy and have your journal and favourite chair ready and inviting.

As you take your seat, I want you to know you are free from distractions for at least the next ten minutes. Settle into a nice rhythm of breathing deeply in through the nose and out through the mouth. As you do this a few times, you'll feel yourself settle into that space within that speaks of peace and harmony. Focus your awareness here, allowing no distractions. Keep breathing and as you do answer this question.

IN MY SENSE OF ONENESS I AM......

This question will bring forth all that you are in the power of love, therefore any thoughts that come to mind that are less than love do not belong here. Fill your journal page with all the loving and inSightful thoughts, feeling and images. There is no right or wrong, no limitations and no judgement in the sacred space of Oneness, so allow this energy to guide you.

Should you find the information not flowing so freely for you, please persist. Use the Soul Conversation each morning as you arise from your sleep and empower yourself each day. One word is all you need to open this door and you will find in time the connection will generate and you will then be able to fill a page of your journal.

Recording this in your journal is a wonderful keepsake to use at times when you need inspiration and nurturing through times of challenge and doubt. That is also a great time to re-do this exercise and if you want a truly powerful experience, then I recommend doing this exercise with a friend or development group, where you share what inSights you receive about one another and who you all are in your sense of Oneness.

If you would like me to walk you through this exercise, then you can receive a download of an audio recording of this exercise by visiting my website.

Recreation

When you begin to experience the soul beyond itself and its connection to the Divine – you begin to understand all that this Universe has to offer. Expanding your thoughts and awareness to embrace the process of recreation and the manifestation of living any incarnation, first begins with exploring your thinking and beliefs on past lives.

My interest in Past Lives began at the beginning of 2007, when I was asked by my

Spirit guides at the time to conduct a Past Life workshop at my spiritual development center, The Australian College of Mediumship. Before this time, I didn't place much value on knowing about your past lives believing they had no real relevance on your current life and all too often, I saw people using them as an excuse for a challenge in this life and not really working towards true healing or personal responsibility with any issue they may have. So while I believed in reincarnation, Past Life Therapy was really something I avoided or left for others to work with.

As you can imagine, I was a little shocked when Spirit asked me to conduct a workshop of this nature. However, as always when I hear from Spirit in this way there really is no possibility of me saying 'No' and not doing as they ask.

This workshop turned out to be one of the most significant life changing moments I've ever experienced and still to this day, is one of my favourite teaching moments.

It began modestly with each of us sharing our thoughts on Past Lives and any experiences we may have had. Before long, it turned into a lively, excitable, discussion prompted by the guided Past Life Meditation I included and what unfolded for me during that.

While guiding the meditation, I took some time to thoroughly sit in the energy and allow Spirit to show me anything they felt I needed to know or experience. In this moment, I was open to all possibilities of new understandings and Spirit saw this opening. Believing as I did in the lack of value or merit in such an integral part of who we are, meant that Spirit felt it right to turn this on its head and nurture the Spirit within me. Spirit recognised I needed this to grow and expand my beliefs of who I am, but they also recognised they needed to unfold this new information in a way that was relatable and totally understood, if I was take hold of it all.

With my work as a psychic medium, I am experienced in the process of trance mediumship which is where the energy of the Spirit world comes in very close and merges with the energy of the medium in an effort to speak through the medium to share their consciousness, thoughts, knowledge and experiences. Spirit took this opportunity during the meditation to have me meet one of my Past Life selves, in the way I would meet and converse clairaudiently (thought transference) with any other Spirit, if I was opening myself up to trance.

This Spirit is a Native American Medicine Woman who over the coming years would step forward at different times revealing a little more of herself while sharing the understandings of how Past Lives are portrayed amidst our very personal connection.

That first night, she shared with me, the view of past lives existing chronologically in order was in fact, not how it is at all, being that time is a man-made construct to create order out of chaos. In unfolding the view, that beyond the time and space dimension we know as Earth, there lies parallel dimensions of realities which hold all the life experiences we have known or are yet to be a part of, all existing simultaneously, alongside on another.

To give you a simple analogy, it's quite like Television. On one channel you have Downtown Abbey airing, I'm loving that show at the moment. While on another you might have the Country Music Channel playing, another favourite he he, with only the aerial frequencies differentiating which channel your TV tunes into. Parallel Lives exist in a similar fashion with only your awareness limiting your knowledge and understanding of their impact on your current life.

Not long after this workshop, as part of the paranormal investigating work I was doing at the time, I visited a run-down abandoned mental health facility in the Blue Mountains region of New South Wales, Australia. In reading the energies of this environment with my

Mediumship ability and connecting with two significant beings, I found the energetic makeup reflecting a fully operational hospital functioning in another dimension. One of the Spirit beings I communicated with was a Doctor who shared with me that his life's work was in researching mental health and to do that, he carried out brain lobotomies on the patients at this facility. This explained the body pit I had psychically connected with a little earlier. He had the most honourable of intentions and in his time he was doing good work. To us it felt like the place was 'haunted' as it would have also felt to the Doctors, nurses and patients when both of our worlds collided in this way, though you could ask who's haunting who? I could however; see Spirit providing me with the experiential validation and life experience I needed to cement my new found beliefs.

More and more there is a growing shift within all of our understanding to accept that our past lives actually exist parallel to one another, operating simultaneously alongside one another in different dimensions of time and space. We are bravely coming to comprehend that the structure of time as we know it, does not apply to the workings of an energetic universe. We are beginning to understand that this is a human need for order out of chaos and know that our true selves, our soul self knows no such boundary. Applying this necessary understanding to the belief of reincarnation means there is no chronological order of your individual past lives, nor is there the perceived limitation of only past lives having existed. Yes, you can access your future lives too!

Imagine yourself as a glowing light of energy, this energy contains a collective group of souls, with you and your current life incarnation being just one of them. To experience a new incarnation the soul breaks away recreating itself in new form taking with it remnants from the soul group, maintaining a deep connection residing within, knowing that at any time the soul can re-join the group and return from whence it came, back to the ether and the collective consciousness.

Each time a soul breaks away to recreate in this way, a wave of evolution unfolds and this energy flows through all those souls connected to the group in this way. This is felt and experienced as emotion, healing and evolution. This same process can be witnessed in the natural world as we see flowers and plants, seed, germinate and grow into new plants. Creating a whole new experience for the reformed energy that becomes the new flower.

When you recognise yourself as a soul first and human second, you begin to understand that life and the mechanics of it, is much bigger than you initially perceive it to be. You understand the connection between yourself and the world you live in, including those you interact with each day. You understand that in living one's truth you give your soul the best chance at being vibrant and enriching to yourself and others while above all else moving through this journey called life, with love. This in itself results in a natural inclination towards positivity, to be generous of Spirit, exhibit empathy towards humanity and to believe that above all else you are a creatively powerful being.

Within you exists an inherent connection to the Divine and All That Is. There is a part of you that is the Spirit world. There is no separation between you, the Divine, the Spirit World or your Parallel Lives. There is only your perception of it.

This then leaves us with the question how do we access this part of who we are? How do you communicate with Spirit? How do you bring through the guidance you need, the love you are and the Spirit you can be on a daily basis.

This process often seems harder than it really needs to be, because we approach it from a place of separation. Even a lot of current metaphysical teaching, especially much of the current teaching of Mediumship and psychic awareness is all based on belief systems of separatism. We see ourselves as humans first and Spirit second, if at all. In addition to not seeing ourselves as part of the Divine or the Spirit world, we see it as being in some other place. Where that is, is different for everyone. I've read books by well-known mediums saying it is three feet above and to the right. This I think comes from the understanding that this is the energetic location of where a spirit will connect to that Mediums energy for the purpose of communication, not really where it really exists.

I know this because this was my experience too! For a long time I believed and taught that the Spirit world was all around me, and to access it with my awareness I always looked above me or behind me. Then with a moment of realisation brought about by new growth and understanding – this belief flew out the window as I came to realise the 'separateness' of living that understanding. That in true essence – 'I am Spirit' and therefore the Spirit world is 'Of' me. With all of me surging forth into the universal energies and consciousness from the core of me, the heart of me. And my connection to it all derives from this very point, from the center of all that is me.

In living from this place of understanding, how then do you expand your awareness to incorporate All That Is.

You first listen to the daily nuances of your own inner voice. You heed the call of your own Spirit. In doing this you keep the noise and confusion to a minimum and therefore allow for the influences of Spirit to seep into your awareness when needed.

If developing an awareness of your soul is new for you, it is imperative to give yourself time in solitude. Find a way that works for you, be it meditation, journaling by the beach or walking with the birds of a morning. Taking time out from the everyday obligations of work, housework and family commitments giving yourself the opportunity to experience oneness with your soul is vitally important to allow the soul to be heard through the noise and clutter of the mind and its daily distractions.

EXERCISE

This exercise will filter into your awareness, the energies of cause and effect for you – highlighted by your choices and how you proceed to implement them in your life.

1. Take the time to listen - spend time in solitude - meditating, journaling or even walking - taking time out from the everyday to hear your inner voice. Consistency is a key here.

2. As you do this, bring your awareness to your heart space and accept all that flows from here for you - being it heartache, pain, confusion or moments of joy and love. Acknowledge and accept.

3. When ready, ask your heart any question you need to and then be prepared to accept

what you receive. Take any action required knowing it will lead you in the direction of freedom, love and healing.

It takes time for this awareness to become a natural part of your everyday without too much thought given to receiving this information, so persist daily and before long you will be a highly attuned expert at aligning with your soul self.

To become aware of all that has existed for you over your span of existence, you must first begin to arouse within you the need to know – to find an innate need to expand yourself and your life in some way, which goes far beyond idol curiosity. For, it is this need that magnetises the experience so that the real magic unfolds for you.

Beauty is only skin deep, while life and all it entails can have you reach far into the depths of the soul, which at times may not be pretty. Imagine leaving on a journey for Santiago, expecting beauty, bliss and sublime beaches only to find derelict buildings, homelessness and a place that had seen better days. Life at times can leave you feeling this way and so too can your journey to visit a Parallel Life. You do need to be prepared for what you may find. Yet, in maintaining your Parallel Life ventures out of need for spiritual understanding, you will ensure you always receive what you need for your soul's evolutionary growth. Harbouring this need will ensure experiences full of answers for you with a high potential for clarity and growth. I urge you to keep this in mind when moving forward with this next exercise.

MEDITATION - Your Soul Self:

Put yourself in your meditation space and give yourself at least the next half an hour free from interruptions and distractions and set the mood with some soft music and lighting.

- Begin with relaxing your body by becoming aware and feeling from within all of your arms and legs, your neck and shoulders and then your back. Feel them gently release any tension that is being held in all of these muscles. If you feel the need to stretch, go with that and let it all go.

- As you feel the body become a little more relaxed, you will now feel more comfortable in your seat.

- Let's take a few deep breaths as you now gently close your eyes.

- With each breath, breathing in through the nose and out through the mouth, you find yourself letting go and sinking further and further into your chair as you release the awareness of the room you are in.

- In this space, you begin to feel lighter and as a wave of energy encroaches from within, you become aware of a presence making themself known to you. This presence feels soft, gentle and inviting while reminding you of your favourite colour. Take a moment to feel the energy of your visitor along with the vibration of colour they bring with them. Feel all that the energy is communicating to you.

- If you find yourself beginning to think a little too much, that's ok. Just remind yourself that now is a time of peace and your mind can return to its ramblings later.

- Feel the Soul within you as this presence – allow it to give itself form. Does your soul self show itself as a male or female? Perhaps neither. How does your soul self look to you? Young, vibrant? Perhaps aged and full of wisdom. Recognise that you inherently know this is your soul self and feel the strength of this oneness.

- Take this opportunity to ask your soul self for some guidance and wisdom, if you need or perhaps use this question.

'Please share with me, what if anything I need to know right now to enhance my life. Thank you.'

- Embrace the warmth that is you, allowing this new awareness to seep its way into your conscious mind. Allowing you to guide yourself now from a greater place of knowing.

- In your own time, you will feel the energy start to lighten and recede. As this happens, slowly start to become aware of your body once again. Become aware of the room you are in and the chair you are sitting on. When you are ready open your eyes.

I would recommend recording your experience in your journal with as much detail as possible. Recognise the information that helps to identify your Soul self. This will assist you to recognise when you receive guidance and insights from your soul self throughout the day or when in meditation.

This meditation is also well suited to use to uncover insightful information centered on the purpose of your current incarnation. By using the following suggested questions during the meditation, they will assist in unfolding the wisdom you are ready to receive.

I would however recommend sitting with this meditation at least three times before using one of these questions. This will allow you the chance to become comfortable with this aspect of your soul affording you the highest potential to achieve your best results.

1. *How can I become more in touch with you?*

2. *How do I stay in this earthly body and do right by you?*

3. *Please share with me, my soul's intention for this lifetime at the point of recreation, thank you.*

4. *Please share with me, any lifetime that is currently having a positive/negative (use one of these) impact on my life at this time.*

5. *I am currently struggling with .... Please share with me any lifetime that can help me to resolve this issue.*

Experiencing a connection to one of your parallel lives through the very real adventure of finding yourself physically visiting the very place where your parallel life is occurring is a phenomenal experience, which besides having far reaching effects on your life, it will fill the holes in your soul, fill your heart with joy and leave you with an undying love for your special place. This is how I feel about Sedona, Arizona. I shared with you earlier and in my first book A New Kind of Normal: Unlock the Medium Within how my first visit to Sedona in 2008 irrevocably changed me forever, just by connecting with the energy of the land. At the time it provided healing and felt glorious, although it raised a lot of questions. Having never experienced anything like this before, I needed answers as to why. What was so special about Sedona? And being told by Spirit it was my 'Spiritual Home' didn't placate me at all. It was however, not until three years later on our return visit in 2011 that the answers would come.

This time I returned with a heightened expectation of wanting to find theses answers and to understand what my connection to Sedona was and why I felt as I did in 2008. Was it a past life connection or was it simply the healing energies that Sedona is well known for.

We had been in the US for a few weeks already with our stop at Sedona being near the end of this trip. It had been a particularly challenging trip, which was making our stop in Sedona all the more enticing. The day we arrived, I booked a full body massage, longing to de-stress and achieve a sense of relaxation.

The massage began much like any other though it didn't take long for me to get lost in the experience and relax enough for the Spirit world to make itself known. This was the moment that as the spirit of a Native American Medicine Woman stepped forward to communicate, I came to the understanding that Sedona was indeed my Spiritual home.

This Medicine Woman explained she was my past life self and that many people feel the call of the Indian and find themselves living or visiting Sedona often. She explained that I would find myself visiting at the end of each significant chapter of soul growth for rest and nurturing of my soul. In fact, this was something I had been doing since childhood when she triggered some memories from long ago. As a child trying to go to sleep at night I often experienced strange energetic happenings, where I would feel on the edge of a chasm, with the feeling of a massive gigantic head and an abrasive feeling, I can only liken to that of sandpaper. These feelings often accompanied picture flashes in my mind of red rock desert, which I now know were clairvoyant experiences. I never spoke of these too anyone, until I began teaching Mediumship and understood the concept of energy. My Spirit friend explained, in this moment that at these times in my life my soul was journeying to Sedona for respite and nurturing. No wonder, I felt such an overwhelming connection to Sedona from the moment I set my foot down on the earth.

We conversed mediumistically for a little while as she shared with me, a little more of herself and therefore myself. When I asked her, her name she showed me a grey stormy night sky with the moon amidst a strong sense of our English language not containing a translation for it. She shared how as a Medicine Woman there were only certain practices in her time a woman could offer. She said she would go beyond this and offer the healing a male medicine man could too, only keeping very quiet and confidential about it. I thought 'That is sooo me!'

She went on to say, while she was unable to read or write she did keep a record of sorts for her patients and this is where I help her. Just as she would appear to me to help when I needed understanding, so too would I appear to her. Together, we are a part of the same soul group experiencing different incarnations alongside one another.

Have you ever thought that this could be where our Spirit Guides come from? In that moment, I certainly understood that this is one form of expression for our guides and how they come to be.

As you can imagine, this download of information was blowing my mind and I was so excited I couldn't restrain myself from sharing it all with the masseuse. Of course, she took it all in her stride being aware of her own calling to Sedona and letting me know that during my massage, she felt as if she was taking part in a Native American campfire ceremony of sorts.

I feel so blessed to have had these magical experiences and to be given such understandings. As I said earlier, visiting your special place will transform your life in many ways. My wish for each and every one of you is for you to visit your spiritual home so you may experience and know a greater part of who you are while rejoicing in the beauty, mystery and magic of somewhere as divine as Sedona.

Part Two

Gifts of the Soul

Your Intuitive Self

"Living from intuition is the result of committing yourself to knowing you are a spark of the Divine Within."

It is through your intuition that your connection to the Divine Consciousness expresses itself. It leads you forward through your sense of knowing, which your intellect will either then reason with or accept the truth of it without question.

In becoming proficient at living from intuition you become more adapt at accepting this truth, allowing a sense of objectivity and recognising when your sense of doubt and fear can cloud your judgement of it all.

Once you lead with objectivity, you allow the will of the Universe and your connection to it, to have its way, instead of trying to override it with a sense of control brought about by your attachment to any desired outcomes. You begin to feel your way through life by putting one foot in front of the other, engaging more in being in the moment. It is these very actions that enable a greater success and the result truly being in alignment with your soul and spiritual destiny.

When the overall design of life does not fit with what you would like life to be, letting go of the way you expect things to be allows your intuition to work more freely, more clearly and more conscisely. It is when you hold tight to expected outcomes that your kicks in along with your control mechanisms, and you try to "fix" it as you see fit, engaging and creating "blocks" within the flow of energy and intuition which are really there by your design anyway.

Becoming a master at living from intuition and the success of living your spiritual destiny always results in a positive outcome. Your soul and spirit knows the purpose and life circumstances which are required to support your destiny and when you are consciously listening to this source of guidance by acting on the intuition, having faith and facing all that is presented before you, how can you not achieve the success that is associated with the path of your spiritual destiny. There is a blueprint, a Soul Contract if you will, that your Soul self is working hard to execute.

Mediumship and communicating with Spirit, for me has been an eighteen year love affair. Throughout that time I have mentored and coached a lot of mediums with my first business, The Australian College of Mediumship and have really developed a unique and very full understanding of how mediumship works.

Imagine my surprise then, when after all this time I heard Spirit say "Your true purpose has not yet been revealed". I had already been following relevant intuition and guidance by closing down classes, I had stopped conducting mediumship readings to focus more on working and educating people to live from the Soul. However, this communication from Spirit still blindsided me, and I'll be honest my immediate response went something like "WTF!!!"

This did however herald a new beginning for me, as Spirit began to drive home the importance of the work I was doing with the Soul and that my true purpose and spiritual destiny lied in combining my working with the Soul and my mediumship to bring about messages and information to others relating to their Soul purpose, which I now call Soul Purpose Mediumship.

I share this story with you to highlight, how easy it is to often expect things to be one way, yet we may not know all the information. So all you can do to be of service to yourself and to others in the best possible way is to learn to listen to your Soul and its sense of intuition, one step at a time.

DEVELOPING INTUITION

As I mentioned earlier the Divine Spirit is expressed through your mind, body and soul by the power of intuition. It is in learning to listen to the subtleties of this that allows you to reap the benefits and empower yourself and your life by making choices guided from this connection to the Divine.

Adrian is a client of mine whom I first met about seven years ago when he was newly diagnosed with a slow growing pancreatic cancer. Through learning to listen to the nuances of his body, Adrian has become highly attuned to the needs of his body and his soul, managing to honour it all by taking the decisive actions necessary. For Adrian, this means being able to successfully and positively manage his cancer from day to day. His intuition works within the framework of Doctor's visits, blood tests, optimising nutrition, exercise and all that Adrian needs to keep living.

This has also lead to a strong and definitive connection to his Spirit, which while still a little unconscious it is a connection that is strong in its ability to communicate the knowledge and guidance needed. Which is what we all want isn't it? Adrian was only recently describing it as this other part of him that rises up with a sense of calmness and he very clearly knows that what is being presented to him is either right or wrong for him. It is particularly powerful for him at times when circumstances may trigger some fear, Adrian says he feels the communication say 'no that's not right for me at this time' and then peace is restored.

Clearly his intuition and Adrian's Spirit is in the driving seat with his life and more importantly his journey with a terminal illness. It is Adrian's commitment to living from intuition and his Spirit that for now sees him well, being with his family and being able to watch his children grow into young adults.

Adrian recently asked how he could make his connection to his Spirit even stronger. My response is now the exercise I share with you here. This simple daily discipline will focus your intention for the day, and as Adrian said make your connection to your Spirit and therefore your intuition much more conscious throughout each day. This begins with listening to your heart and soul, and following through with the actions required. It is this act of following through with action that clears the way to greater clarity and a more in tune connection to your guidance source.

Most of us begin consciously waking to our spirituality in times of need, so it is possible that you may feel lost, confused and hurting, leaving the energy of your soul clouded. This cloudiness is a hinderance to receiving clear communication, much like trying to talk through cotton wool. The clearer we can be with our energy the greater capacity we have to receive a clear and conscise communication. There are many things that go into entangling our soul in cloudiness, such as our emotional baggage, negativity, judgement and more but once we begin to live our truth and honour who we truly are in each moment, the light of your Divine Spirit begins to show itself and guides us to work towards clearing all that gets in the way of this light shining. Living from intuition is nothing but living from Divine Spirit, or living with God.

Therefore the first step to developing your intuition is to make a commitment to living from the Divine Spirit within your Soul. To do this well it requires an awareness of your heart, mind, body, soul and spirit. In essence a greater conscious awareness of all that you are.

To bring this about let's begin each day with a little Soul Conversation.

EXERCISE

As you wake each morning from your slumber, but before you start to arise and have put your feet on the floor, lie there for a few more minutes and ask yourself this question.

"What is it that my Spirit needs today?"

Opening the channel to communicate daily with your Soul in this way will see you inSpired with thoughts, feelings, clairvoyant imagery and more as your Spirit works at answering your question. Over the years I've received a wide variety of answers from "Rest", which I love as I can lull about home with permission from Spirit alleving any guilt I may feel, to "Intimacy" which usually means hubby's going to get lucky. Or there are the times I have a sense of expansion, conflict or times I hear I need some 'heart' meaning I need to give a little that day.

If you need some initial help to receive your wisdom, simply hold your hand over your heart as you ask the question.

Remember though, the key here is to follow through on any actions that may identify themselves. For example, speaking up and expressing yourself if need be or working towards change because your Spirit is inhibited by the job you live with. All of this will be highlighted through the simple act of asking your Spirit what it needs. In doing so, you are giving yourself a key to greater things like the key to discovering your spiritual destiny. What it is you are here on this earth to do and what it is you need to love more.

From time to time, I also change the question around a little to suit my needs, so here are a couple of other questions you will also find helpful.

"What is it, I need to know for today?"

"What can I do today that moves my life/ my connection to Spirit forward?" (Choose one option)

As you work with this on a daily basis, you will experience an increase in your intuition making itself known more throughout your day. Your conscious awareness will be more heightened, until it becomes more natural for you, so remember that many times throughout the day, your Intuition will show itself through your feelings, your thoughts and not to mention your "hunches". Then in time you will become more disciplined at understanding your mind and the content of your thoughts, being able to distinguish the with its thoughts of fear and doubt to that of your Spirit and you will in time find the mind blending seamlessly with intuition to become One.

Once you have a greater sense of Oneness within, which is mirrored by your connection to ALL That Is, the mind and intuition work more in unison, with your intuitive thoughts really being no different to any other thought you may encounter. Over time and with experience there is no need to differentiate between an intuitive thought and your usual thoughts because it is all part of the whole and who you are. You would have worked hard to provide your intuition with a strong voice and have proven to your self, that it is a reliable source time and time again, leaving you to question and doubt less and less each time, while your faith in your intuition is expanding and growing all the while.

Embracing the Ego

                        The biggest hindrance to developing and living your intuition is our own ego. According to the dictionary Ego is defined as:

Ego the Self, especially as distinct from the world and other selves. While in terms of psychoanalysis it is the division of the psyche that is conscious, most immediately controlling thought and behavior, and is most in touch with external reality.

This signifies all of your conscious self, that part of you that knows and understands you exist as a separate individual within this world, and to continue this existence you Ego must always see itself as separate. It must see that you drive a blue car, that you enjoy moments of hysteria when following your passion and that you love your family and friends more than you love life itself, your neighbours or people you have yet to meet. However, this striving to remain separate creates an inherent insecurity which underlies all that we do. Through fear and judgement we integrate into this world from the time we are born, creating a life that validates the Ego and its need for seperateness. Collectively, this is what we are conditioned too, especially in western society where our sense of the Divine Spirit is often left at the door.

Yet if you take a moment to fully appreciate the true definition of Ego you would understand that Ego in its completeness is a mix of good and bad, positive and negative, light and dark. That it embraces all of the great traits that is you, so much as it does the traits you would prefer did not exist. Your intelligence, your loyalty, your sense of adventure and your willingness to please beyond what is good for you, your negative self talk, your like for drama and your ability to hold yourself back through fear of moving forward.

This then begs the question as to why our experience of the Ego, especially with current spiritual teachings largely highlights the negative. Why is it that we associate Ego as fear, doubt, self importance and all the traits we don't like about ourselves or perceive we need to change when its true purpose is to help us make sense of the world we live in, helping us to individualise our journey here on the earth plane which is the whole point of existence really. As I see it, essentially the Ego is a vital element in one's spiritual journey and our path to evolution.

When you understand the Ego as an inherent part of who you are, embracing it and working towards balancing its voice with that of your

Divine Spirit you then alleviate the pressure you put on ourself to change therefore allowing yourself to move towards self acceptance with far more ease and grace. It is in this act of self acceptance and loving yourself as God loves you, that magic truly exists. When peace and happiness can really come to the fore as you let go of trying to 'fix' everything you don't like about yourself or your life.

This doesn't mean you shouldn't strive to be more loving or a fuller expression of who you are, nor does it mean you shouldn't have an awareness of your Ego. Absolutely you should. Life will flow much more smoothly if you operate as an observer and can effectively say to yourself *"Oh I see you Ego and I understand why. I do love you however I serve my best interests if I do as my Spirit wishes and not listen to you so much"*.

In time you will learn to lessen your attachment to the ego and really find yourself much more in balance with your Soul self as the presence of your Ego and Divine Spirit align in harmony.

So how do you become a little more intimate with this aspect of yourself? How do you embrace it? Ego is largely conflicted or triggered into action by fear and a sense of feeling threatened. Ego says "Ah ha, I know how this feels and in the past it hasn't worked out so well, so I'm going to act out and protect you by stopping you from going there"

The power for you to lessen this kind of impact in your life lies in acknowledging your behaviours in your life that have a base in fear, doubt and ego and to identify your personal triggers which can spark the ego into action. In years gone by before my self awareness is what it is today, I would easily find myself spiralling with negative thought patterns, beating up on myself and questioning all that I am. All because one of my triggers had presented in life, such as having someone think ill of me and my work or feeling less than for not having enough money. These could easily see me head into a dark cloud of energy with an uphill battle to come back from. This very pattern had me moving two steps forward and one step back my whole life and just constantly going around in circles.

It wasn't until I gained full appreciation for my Divine Spirit and came to my knees with self acceptance that I began to turn things around, seeing in even greater detail how my Ego was getting in the way. The key though was not trying to change this about myself, but accepting it as being part of who you are. This act of self love is the simple act that allows the awareness of what is occurring to rise to your conscious mind and therefore give you the power to choose your next step. Which of course, will be an act based in love.

With the intention to assist you to raise your awareness of when the negative aspects of your ego are at play in your life holding you back, here is a handy checklist to help you identify its presence. Please note, these attributes are all common experiences however this list is in no way complete. Please allow for your own individual experiences as well.

- Inability to move forward or procrastination.
- Stomach tightness or knots.
- Questioning and doubting everything about yourself.
- Anxiety and nervousness.
- Not being able to focus on anything.
- Your mind starts to go into overdrive.
- Dark clouds of depression start to descend.
- Easily distracting yourself.
- Emotionally sensitive.
- Moodiness.

TRIGGER TRAPS

Recognising your own trigger traps is powerful beyond measure. It is in doing this that you are able to say to yourself *"I see what is going on, and I'm not going to fall for this again"*. As I mentioned earlier, I have two major triggers, being judged unkindly by others and not having enough money to do all that I want to do, both of which I have worked very hard at over the years to lessen my Ego's attachment to. These triggers while personal to me, I'm sure could be relevant for you too. At the heart of all of us, we are no different to one another. Each of us want to be liked and accepted by others and many of us find that money, wealth and abundance is something we find hard to come by. Your triggers can be set off so easily into some of the above behaviours, which then starts the spiralling process of disconnecting you from your Divine Spirit. The power to stop this occurring lies in recognising this happening first and foremost.

Below please take some time to list what you believe some of your triggers are. If you find that hard to do, think back to the last time you experienced fear and doubt and some of the behaviours above. Ask yourself with honesty, "What do I believe caused me to behave this way?" and if you need extra help please ask your Divine Spirit, your higher self, your guides, your Angels, God or whatever guidance source you work with to help. Allow them to show you.

MY TRIGGER TRAPS

1.

2.

3.

4.

Now that you've recognized that the Ego is acting out in fear and doubt, causing some angst and behaviours that are not serving you. What can we do to shift the focus, let go and get back on track?

Here is my offer of assistance. I recommend doing these in order, so be kind to yourself and:

1. Whatever it is you are doing – STOP.

Let go of your to do list - just for a little while.

2. Acknowledge

Give yourself time to hear the Soul Speak.

Take your journal and acknowledge out loud your doubts and fears even if you don't fully understand them.

Being honest with yourself, holding it all with awareness means you are half way through it already.

3. Revitalise

Do something to re-invigorate yourself.

Take a Ferris Beuller day off.

Visit the beach or spend time in nature.

Go shopping or to the gym.

Connect with supportive people who inSpire you.

Lastly, I offer you this meditation to also assist in bringing you back to your Divine Spirit and its sense of Oneness, overriding all Ego and allowing the energy of love to once again be the Divine hand guiding your being and therefore your life.

MEDITATION – *Journey to Oneness*

Allow yourself the time and space needed to complete this meditation of approximately twenty minutes. I encourage you to establish a little corner in your favourite room which is quiet and

you know you won't be disturbed. Trust that you will feel drawn to the right space when keeping the intention of meditating on your mind.

Here, make your meditation space as comfortable as possible with some gentle music, soft lighting or candles and generous smells of oils and incense wafting about. Include whatever you feel is needed to make it 'home'. Your chair should be comfortable with enough room to allow you a straight back which enables the flow of your energy.

As you sit comfortably, first begin by taking a few deep breaths. In through the nose and out through the mouth. Allow yourself the space here for the natural flow of your breath, just taking it a little deeper than you normally would.

- With each breath focus on drawing in some beautiful universal energy and visualise this energy in all its rainbow coloured glory, filling your body with its mesmerising self.

- Begin with feeling this energy come in with your breath and find its way into your chest. Here it begins to awaken and tingle the heart center with its gentle caress before it continues onward.

- The energy slowly starts to find itself guided by where its needs to go most to naturally balance your energy. Pay close attention to how this feels for you.

- In your own time you will become aware that this glorious rainbow of energy now needs to specifically work more through your energy centers, aligning you to the Divine. Please begin by visualising a new column of light coming up through the floor and entering your body through the soles of your feet connecting and grounding you to Mother Earth. This column of light will be a colour specific to you, providing you with what is needed right now.

- As you feel this energy around your feet, you sense it begin to move up through your legs as it finds its way to your Base chakra, positioned at the base of your spine. Feel this energy center start to transform and awaken while becoming aware of what thoughts transpire for you at this point. This gives you a good inSight into the functioning and healing required around this energy center.

- Upwards your beautiful column of light continues to travel, finding its way to your Sacral chakra which is just below your navel. Here, the energy aligns itself with your sexuality and adolescence awakening within you all that you are. Again, take heed of any thoughts that intervene and make a mental note to recall them later.

- The Solar Plexus chakra is the next to be stimulated by this omnipresent power of life force energy. Feel your center expand with new life as your Solar Plexus, situated just below the breast bone becomes alive with energy. As with the two previous chakras, acknowledge and let go of the thoughts which arise.

- The Heart center is where it began and now you find it begins to soften with empathy and understanding as the energy transforms your heart chakra into awareness and the power of love.

- Take a few minutes here to enjoy and feel all that is in your heart.

- In your own time, the energy and its cascading colour will continue upwards to redefine your Throat chakra, allowing you to express yourself like never before. As you find the glow of light healing any inhibitions and stimulating this energy center. Acknowledge any thoughts that arise again and ask to be reminded later.

- With the flow of energy nearing its peak, the column of light seeks out your brow or third eye chakra leaving you in no doubt that this is the seat of great clarity as much as it is the seat of all judgement. Allow the energy to align this center with purity of Spirit to bring about any much needed clarity. Be aware of your thoughts at this point, acknowledge them, let them go and find the resulting sense of peace that awaits.

- Relax even more and take some more time to revel in the rewards of this inner sojourn.

- All energy has its own consciousness and with the last leg of this journey, your column of light begins its way to your Crown chakra and out through the top of your head, where this energy enhances your connection to the Divine. Allowing a greater sense of All That Is, to creep into your consciousness hurling you forward into that great expanse of Oneness. Knowing that all of life is intimately connected and that we are all one, brings with it a greater sense of self and an ever increasing awareness of All That Is. This is the gift you give yourself today.

- Allow yourself some time to BE.

- In your own time, you will feel the energy start to lighten and recede. As this happens, slowly start to become aware of your body once again. Become aware of the room you are in and the chair you are sitting on. When you are ready open your eyes and see your new world.

- Perhaps you may like to take some time now to record your experience in your journal, while enjoying a nice quiet cup of tea or coffee.

One last thought on embracing the Ego, currently we largely live in an Ego centered world where the Collective Consciousness is still honouring the Ego above that of the Divine Spirit. On an individual level this can be challenging as we personally grow to greater depths with Spirit yet are required to interact daily with people who to varying degrees still operate egoically. This can be especially difficult when it is those you love and who you spend a lot of your time with.

You may find this a big challenge the more you become aware of your own Ego and seeing it reflected in your closest relationships. This at times will have you feeling powerless and like you are banging our head up against a brick wall. Consciously, we desire to operate in this world with all interactions being based in love, yet there are times when this world and others in it seem to have a stronger hold. So in asking my higher self to offer you something that will make a difference here for you, I hear this prayer.

"I ask the Divine light of God to walk before me this day, so that my life may flow with ease and grace. Thank you"

Naturally Psychic

When you know and understand the Divine Spirit within is connected to all things and all people throughout all time and space this will leave you with no energetic boundaries or limitations and the ability to communicate in Spirit then becomes a natural process.

By living from a deep sense of Oneness with all creation, the power is within you to know all. Whether it be from the past, present or future of this life time, the hollows of another time and dimension or the whispers of one's Spirit since passed. Your capacity as a Medium is only limited by what you understand or believe the process to be and by opening your mind and your heart a little you can redefine who you are and learn to communicate spiritually in new ways.

Clairvoyance, Clairaudience and Clairsentience (the 3C's) are the three most commonly accepted forms of psychic ability, which traditionally have come about through a process of separation. Whereby we believe that to communicate with the Spirit world or the energy of another, we do so separately and as individuals living on the earth plane. And yes, this is the physical reality, however it is not the spiritual reality.

The Spiritual reality has us all existing as one collective consciousness, which we all individually contribute to with our awareness, our energy and our sense of being. It is in this space where your energetic antennae, has the capacity to tune in and pick up the relevant signals. Doing this with a solid belief and knowing that you as a human exist as Spirit form first and foremost enables you a more free flowing distinguishable communication process. One, that resides within and allows all of the information to flow from here, no longer in separation and clearly more discernable. Gone are the old ways of trying to interpret messages with great gusto, as you are left with a process of psychic and mediumistic communication that is as natural as breathing.

I wrote extensively about developing the 3C's in my first book A New Kind of Normal: Unlock the Medium Within so I won't go over it too much here except to give you the basics.

Clairvoyance – is the ability to see with your heart

Clairaudience – is the ability to hear through the mind

Clairsentience – is the ability to feel the truth with your soul

Understanding these aspects of your psychic ability is worthwhile to lay a foundation and build upon with new knowledge. However, please don't get too caught up in them and which one works best or is a struggle for you. It is not like you think too much about using any of your human senses of sight, touch or hearing as you go about your day and the same can be said with your psychic ability.

The 3C's do all work in conjunction with one another helping to complete the picture of communication for you. We are all Clairvoyant, Clairaudient and Clairsentient to varying degrees which when nurtured and developed can greatly extend upon your intuition and provide a solid foundation for spiritual awareness and a reliable tool to receive wisdom and guidance. It really can be a natural process and one that only needs to be awakened and attuned in a way that allows for this.

Having personally migrated from a total lack of psychic ability to being a fully functioning Medium with an ability now centered in Oneness, I partly attribute to allowing me to not only validate the continued existence of the consciousness of your loved ones, but to also access information regarding their and your Soul purpose, giving you a greater understanding of why you and your life came to be. Over the last eighteen years, I have travelled the road of developing, nurturing and finetuning my psychic awareness. It does take time, commitment and discipline but is totally worth any challenge you may face with it.

Over the years as a mentor and coach for Mediumship development I have come across many, many people from all walks of life who have awakened their ability to communicate in Spirit. In all that time the only people I have seen incapable of receiving any form of communication are the ones who are really challenged with having an open heart. Communicating in Spirit with the Spirit of another is a very intimate process, so those of you, who through hurt are not willing to allow others to get close, to trust others with your heart or open up and express who you are will struggle. This is true for everyone to a certain degree, however it is your willingness and consistency to work through this that can make all the difference. I know you can do it, otherwise you wouldn't be reading this book. And knowing the benefits of peace, JOY and happiness first hand from walking that journey, I know you deserve it too.

DEVELOPING PSYCHIC ATTUNEMENT

I've written this book with the intention that it benefits you with your personal connection to your Divine Spirit, not to provide you with experience or understanding that is required for a professional psychic or medium. It is recommended that if you are seeking to work as a professional intuitive in any capacity that you find a good mentor who aligns with your values and is practicing the modality you are looking for. For example, you cannot learn mediumship from someone who largely practices Tarot. Secondly, professional Mediumship is something you are called to do, it is a soul urge and as such defines who you are, not just what you do. My experience has seen many start out on this road only to find themselves end up somewhere else entirely, so remember it is about following your guidance while allowing for what needs to be for you and your soul purpose, which will be an entirely different purpose to mine or another mediums such as John Edward.

Your own Soul is the instrument and tool of choice here. There is no greater source of wisdom than the connection between two Spirits of the Divine consciously merging as one for the intended purpose to be of service for the greater good of another.

The law of attraction states that like attracts like, and in the process of mediumship this is also true. To receive the clearest of information for the highest good of another you as the instrument need to be the clearest and of the highest good you can be possibly be at all times, but especially before you intend to offer intuition, psychic information or mediumship to another.

If your energy is shrouded with anger, resentment, alcholol, drugs or anything that is detrimental to your own state of being this can impact not only how well the process works , from how clearly you receive information to the kinds of information you'll receive. One of my former students, Jacinta had a keen interest in crime investigation novels, murder and crime which led to attracting very similar discarnates from the Spirit world. This of course can be interesting work as a professional but when you are learning to ground and balance yourself as a developing medium it can be very off putting and can serverely unbalance your life.

This law of attraction will even show itself with your emotional issues and can easily influence a reading or the information received. I recall watching one particular medium work a gallery style event where every reading contained information regarding the recipients personal relationship. Were they currently in a relationship? Was it going to last? The thing was most of the information was inaccurate and not helpful to the people receiving the message. My summation here was that the medium needed to attend to whatever it was in her life regarding her own personal relationship area and gain the ability to be more clear and objective.

A lot of psychics would recommend the use of visualisations before opening up energetically to receive psychic communication such as the using white light to clear, ground and protect our energies. Whereas I personally prefer and recommend to live every moment of every day knowing that I am a being of light and love. Living with the knowing that you are light, that you are Divine Spirit is the most natural form of protection there is, leaving you with no need to call it in from somewhere outside of yourself because in your sense of Oneness and connection with All That Is, it already exists within.

With a connection to the Spirit world that is honoured from within there really is no need for the traditional practice of meditating to raise your vibration to meet the Spirit world and have Spirit lower their vibration to meet yours. Knowing you are Spirit with no boundaries or limitations who truly understands that the Spiritual reality exists only with a sense of Oneness, allows you to communicate just as you are with your natural vibration.

Yes, before you embark on any form of work on behalf of the Divine Spirit, I do recommend a meditation or small visualization to center and balance yourself, so you let go of what is on your mind leaving you aligned with your Divine Spirit within and can ensure you are solely focused on the highest intention with your friend and/or recipient. Personally, I also take this opportunity to set and affirm my intention for making the connection while also offering a prayer of thanks and gratitude for the opportunity to be of service. I suggest finding the visualization, prayer or ritual that is right for you to align yourself with the Divine Spirit within, though here is an offering you may find helpful.

EXERCISE

Creative visualisation for communicating with Spirit:

Please find yourself a comfortable spot where you know you will be undisturbed for approximately 15 minutes. Allow yourself to feel calm and at peace by playing some relaxing music and burning incense or candles to induce the appropriate atmosphere.

- As you find yourself seated in your favourite chair, close your eyes and take three deep breaths.

- With each breath, breathe in through the nose and out through the mouth, taking each breath a little deeper.

- Feel yourself relaxing a little more into your chair.

- With the body fine tuning itself to the task ahead, I want you to Imagine a stream of white light pouring itself in through the bottom of your feet. This energy is pure, contains great clarity and in its infinite wisdom is free from all judgment. It knows only love.

- As this energy slowly makes it's way up your legs and into your body, you begin to feel loved. Each and every ounce of you is feeling pure love.

- You recognise this and as the energy finds its way to the core of your being, you find yourself feeling centered, empowered and at the heart of your true self.

- Take a moment to feel the full expression of this.

- In its own time the energy continues to move and filters through your upper body. Firstly, your shoulders and then into your head where it stimulates the energy centers associated with your clairvoyance and your clairaudience.

- As it moves upward through your Crown chakra, the scenery within your minds' eye begins to change and you find yourself on a beach, walking on the sand along the waters edge.

- You hear the sound of the waves crashing in. You feel the gentle breeze and the warmth of the suns' rays as you relish in this moment.

- Looking around, you notice a figure walking towards you from the other end of the beach.

- As they come closer, you are not surprised to recognise who it is, for you know within you this whole exercise is for them. They need your intuitive guidance, your wisdom and healing.

- As they near, ask yourself "What is it they need to know and hear right now? How can I help them?"

- Feel the presence of their Soul as it meets with yours, embrace it with love and take a moment to receive the answer as together you walk along the beach in communion and connection. Enjoying the full appreciation of this moment of love.

- In Divine time, you begin to feel the energy fade and recognise it is time to begin saying goodbye to your friend. As they return back along the beach, take a moment to put your feet in the water allowing it to caress you, cleanse your energies and bring you back to your body.

- Slowly, the imagery begins to dissipate and you find yourself back in your room. Aware of your body, wriggling your fingers and toes and in your own time opening your eyes.

This meditation will work for you no matter your level of experience with psychic awareness. Should this be a new experience for you, please be open to receiving information in a variety of ways. It is often a subtle feeling, a flash of an image or thoughts that you may think are your own. Trust this is not the case, as you have asked for guidance and the Spirit is responding. I expect a wide variety experiences for you in meeting your friend on the beach. You may find that your friend turns out to be someone you know, a family member, your Spirit guide, a loved one who has passed away or even a version of yourself. There really is no limitation, so please trust and allow the Divine Spirit to guide the process. And if your first efforts only reveal a little something leaving you unsure, try not to be disappointed. This can be expected, so keep persisting. In time the connections will grow, expand and before long you will be delightfully surprised.

At completion of your meditation, I highly recommend recording your experience and its outcomes in your journal. Firstly, so you have accurate recall for when relaying this guidance with your friend and second, over time you will see your own growth and progress.

Lastly, here is my tip if you are a developing psychic or medium who works with others on a regular basis. This visualisation will be very effective when incorporated as part of your ritual at the commencement of conducting any psychic or mediumship reading.

Your Creative Spirit

As part of the Divine Spirit the creative heart is one that knows JOY.

Creativity is the spark of life. It resides within each of us forming an underlying base that is all of life. When you create from the heart, giving rise to your ideas, your wants and desires as you see them come to fruition and manifest into reality it brings with it a sense of accomplishment, which is accompanied by feelings of pure JOY. One of the greatest gifts this life has to offer is the ability to express yourself with creativity.

We do this with all manner of avenues from art, music and design, to every moment of every day with all of life. It is this power within, your Divine Spirit that gives birth to the career or job you work in each day, the friends you attract, the relationships you find yourself in and the moment to moment choices you make each day. Most things may be considered unconscious choices and yes, there is a lot that occurs you wouldn't choose in a month of Sundays, they are however still creative choices brought about by the creative energy you walk with that powers this process.

Each of us are born with an individual set of life circumstances and experiences designed to support your Soul purpose and its desire for evolution. Given that the Soul's intention is to evolve into the best expression of itself that it can be, how it chooses to execute this intention is the very fabric of why each of us are so different while providing each of us with a unique Spiritual Destiny and pathway to life. It is the reason you are born to a particular country and also the family dynamic you find yourself connected to.

Your Divine Spirit is the guiding force, the Soul's compass if you will, keeping you on track and in alignment with your Soul's evolutionary intention and pre-birth plan. This occurs whether you realise it or not and shows itself when moments of Destiny are employed to try and help you engage or re-align with this pathway.

There is, of course many a person who choses not to engage these moments of Destiny which head you toward discovering your purpose in life. Some find it too confronting a challenge while others are more comfortable with what they already know. For me, it was not even a choice. After my brother's death from suicide nearly twenty years ago, the need within me to find more meaning for my life was too great not to recognize it and ignoring it wasn't even possible. So when the moment came for me to read The Celestine Prophecy by James Redfield and have the spark of the Divine ignite within me, it was a moment of recognition. A moment where I appreciated that there was more to life than just existing with a nine to five job and a new baby. That my brother had given me one of the greatest gifts a soul can give another. He gave me the gift of spiritual awakening.

Shaking off the stronghold of the Ego enough to know that within the depths of who we are lies the true essence of the Divine in all its glory, intuition, wisdom, consciousness, awareness and creativity. Perhaps between my brother and I there lies a soul agreement for this very purpose which I am yet to fully comprehend and know. Whether it exists or not, I am eternally grateful that for this gift Allen gave me. I can only hope that I have gone on to give meaning and purpose to his life and the pain it contained for him. He is a big part of my work and he does make his presence known from time to time, not just to me but also to others as he guides, protects and remains invested in wanting to help others.

As I pause with the writing here, thinking about what is to come next I sense a block in the energies and know this relates to the flow of creativity in life as much as it does writing this chapter. I feel the presence of the block give way to truth as I acknowledge this and the block lifts to reveal what lies beneath. Connection and truth, and as I allow this to seep forward my heart no longer hurts with grief from what I just wrote regarding my brother.

Underlying any conscious effort to create is the Soul's purpose and your prebirth plan. Therefore when you work at manifesting your dreams and heart desires you have greater success in achieving them when they are aligned with your Soul's purpose. When your goals are derived from within, seated in the truth of who you are as unique spark of the Divine, the universe will support your efforts much more willingly with ease and grace. As opposed to momentus effort for little return where you feel constantly bereft of achieving and just banging your head up against a brick wall trying to achieve goals rooted in trying to fix a problem.

Finding it within yourself to listen, to hear what the heart and soul wants is the first step to successfully creating. This requires giving yourself some time away from the to-do list and distractions or responsibilities of life. Let's begin simply by using this daily Soul Conversation to allow the soul to speak.

"What is it that my heart and soul desires me to do to be happy/or to make a difference in this world......"

At times you will find this flows more fluently than other times, so too do the universal energies of flow and creativity. It is in these moments of lull and downtime that you are best to use them productively to re-energise, review, re-evaluate and check in with yourself to see if your desires and future directions need changing because you have personally have changed and therefore have new needs and desires.

Adjusting the sails is a necessary part of the creative process. When you sit to create a set of goals and focus on your directions this is essentially what you are doing. You are listening and readjusting. Life never has you not moving forward without intention. You are now just becoming a more aware and conscious player in this game of life.

GAINING CLARITY

Leading you forward, I find the best way to obtain clarity is to clear emotion first. Any emotion that is old, stale and holding you back is best acknowledged, out in the open giving it the best chance to be let go of and in the interest of keeping it simple, please take your journal, align yourself in Oneness and answer these four questions.

My achievements and all that I am grateful for are: (Please list them).

What is it that is not working for me in my life right now?

From this list, what is it I need to let go of, if anything?

What is it I can transform right now? And how do I start this process?

TAKING YOUR CREATIVITY A LITTLE DEEPER

Keep working with your journal, only now lets turn your focus to going forward by answering this question. The nature of this Soul Conversation will inSpire responses from a deeper part of who you are, so please just trust in the process and allow whatever flows onto the page.

My life flows from Oneness and the Wisdom of my Soul is creating...

The intention here is for you to create a picture of all that you desire you life to be. However, the pictures, ideas and thoughts of it are coming to mind for you to take action, while the creation of it all lies within your Soul Self and the Spirit where you want it to be. While writing all that inspires you, please be sure to include how it will all feel when you are living your dream. This is important for you to expand the connection from within to the future you are creating, helping you to stay connected in times of doubt.

Setting your goals is not enough to see them become a reality. It is imperative to follow through with action and one of the most effective ways to do this and lead yourself forward into success is to be aware of how you spend your time each day. Your daily choices can either circumvent your goals by being mutually exclusive when weighted to heavily towards obligation and responsibility. Remember Cheryl from earlier in the book? Her daily choices where thwarting her aim of staying spiritually connected. Or you can consciously align your daily choices and how you spend your time. For example, for me to achieve the goal of writing this book it is vital that one of my daily priorities is to write. Not always easy to do.

I do often find this a challenge amongst the needs of family, earning an income, clients and publishing inSpirit Magazine but unless I have the right mindset and make the goal a priority in life it is not likely to happen. It is not just going to materialise out of thin air, even if I do think it is a miracle in itself. Remember by shifting the priority and making room to work on creating the goal, you are also making room for the new reality that achieving the goal brings to your life.

Be aware that "where attention goes reality follows". Meaning that what you give most of your attention and energy to becomes your reality. This is especially important when one is focused on negativity or the fact that life is not how you want it to be. Focusing on the lack will see your creative energy going into that, and thereby creating more lack. Instead, choose to focus on what it is you are aiming to create, what makes your heart sing and therefore your creative energy will fuel this.

This is why the setting of your daily choices which are aligned with your heart centered goals is so important. By keeping it simple and focusing on how you spend your time each day, it leaves you free to be in the moment while your co-creative energy powers along fuelled by the JOY you are experiencing from living the heart centered daily choices you have given yourself.

Yes, of course those daily choices realistically need to incorporate your family needs, earning a living and all the other tasks associated with living in a modern world. Though unless you are a little self aware to incorporate your needs and wants too, life will continue to flow along as it always has. And while I am sure there is much in your life for you to be grateful for, I also know you were drawn to read this book because your Soul is seeking change in some way.

TIPS FOR CREATING HEART CENTERED GOALS, INTENTIONS AND DAILY CHOICES.

- Believe that you are worthy of all that you desire.

- Trust that it will all flow to you from the highest source.

The above points on believing and trusting where given to me from the highest source within me, for you. God wants you know this right now!

And now its over to the practicalities.

- Center yourself and align yourself with your Divine Spirit within. Use whatever technique you desire to create this awareness in the moment. If you need assistance then the Journey to Oneness meditation in the previous chapter will help.

- Take your journal and review the previous Soul Conversation just completed, where you described your life as it is in Oneness.

- Take a moment to sit with the energy this Soul Conversation has created for you and now extend upon this by selecting the goals you see for yourself here.

- Create goals that touch all areas of your life. Doing this helps to maintain balance and keep life on an even keel, so create at least one goal for each of these areas in your life.

    Personal growth
    Home
    Health
    Career
    Financial
    Family

Social
Leisure
Others

- Next, inspire yourself with the idea of how life would look on a daily basis when you have achieved these goals and create your daily choices from here.

Remember your goals, intentions and daily choices are created from a deep desire within, a Soul urge to do good in this world. Try to refrain from creating them from a need to fix a problem. This will only generate more negativity, where as focusing on the need within will expand life from a place of JOY, compassion and understanding.

A LITTLE MORE ACCEPTANCE

The desire within us to create is a strong one when we live a soul centered life, yet is often perplexing to find that the ideals we hold for achieving our goals often do not match the reality. Why is that? What is really occurring on a soul level while we are thinking that our goals and hearts desires may never come to be.

Firstly the Divine Spirit would have you work towards accepting where you are at right now. Accepting who you are and all that you are becoming, for in doing so you give yourself the gift of self acceptance. Loving yourself just for who you are right now and in the way God wants you to love yourself.

Why then is achieving our goals so intrinsically tied to acceptance? On the surface it looks like it doesn't it? Though in actuality, acceptance is not tied to achieving your goal at all. However until you see yourself for who you truly are and as the someone you goal says you are, you truly cannot go on to give to others wholehearted until you have achieved this for yourself. For example, if your goal is to be a highly sought after business coach helping people to create wealth, you cannot achieve the heights of this goal until you have learnt all there is to know to help others and have achieved wealth for yourself, perhaps even more than once after your business faulters. It is only then that your authenticity and knowledge will be a lighthouse for others. For me, as a soul coach who educates others on the know how of living from the soul and seeing yourself for who you truly are, my success was limited until I truly saw myself in the way God wanted me to see myself. I needed to see myself for the light that I am, to value my wisdom, knowledge and mediumship as I value others and until such time as I did what I was teaching was really about teaching myself first.

Until you achieve this, the goal cannot be come a reality though what you are doing is walking the path towards goal achievement. You are taking action and manifesting your new reality, only there is more to achieving this goal than you fully comprehend. As you walk this path, you are learning, growing and changing yourself into the person you need to be to live the reality associated with your goal.

Acceptance of the journey as it needs to be leads you to achievement must faster than trying to counter act or control it with resistance. Acceptance will free the creative flow of energy, allowing all that needs to come to you to move you forward. My own journey can best illustrate how this works. There have been plenty of time in my life where I could have embraced Acceptance more fully, making life easier and the road to actualising my goals a little quicker that's for sure.

Eight years ago I began inSpirit Magazine after being inspired by Spirit in answer to my desire for an opportunity to write for a magazine. My Ego self as is the nature of the Ego quickly assigned expectation to this project and over the years I have constantly sought to grow the circulation and readership. Quite a normal expectation for a magazine, wouldn't you say, and a measure of success for any magazine. There have been many a time when I have drawn the line in the sand, putting my foot down with the universe saying *"enough is enough"* after years of funding the magazine, making no money and missing the point.

It has taken me all these years to let go of that measure and accept that behind the surface there are other factors involved. Success can be measured in many ways and over the years inSpirit Magazine has been the avenue through which many of our contributors have given birth to the writer within. We have created a community that supports, cherishes and celebrates the work, not just of our contributors but of many, many people within the world wide spiritual community whether they be New York Times best selling authors or someone who is just beginning their journey of sharing their unique wisdom publicly. It is hard to see this kind of success if all you are looking at is where your creative project is not hitting your ideal mark, yet when you do take a moment of objectivity and realign with its course of success, not just the course of success of assign to it, you then begin to understand its soul purpose. This then allows for the hidden gems and miracles of synchronicity that hold the growth and expansion to reveal themselves.

MEDITATION FOR ACCEPTANCE

This meditation will move towards aligning you with the soul purpose of any hearts desire you feel is not where you want it to be. Forcing it will not bring it closer, however if you open yourself, free of expectation and allow your heart's desire to reveal its true self to you, then you gain a greater understanding behind the hidden purpose and meaning of it coming to be. This knowledge then empowers you into acceptance and allows you to move forward with greater awareness of the soul of that which you are creating.

Before you begin please take a moment to set the intention for what it is you are seeking greater alignment with. For example, in staying with my magazine project, my intention would read...

"Please help me to align my vibration and the vibration of inSpirit Magazine, so that it serves its soul purpose while growing and expanding to reach thousands of people. Please reveal to me in a way I understand, what it is I need to know to match this vibration and achieve this, thank you".

Please find yourself a comfortable spot where you know you will be undisturbed for approximately 20 minutes. Allow yourself to feel calm and at peace by playing some relaxing music and burning incense or candles to induce the appropriate atmosphere.

- As you find yourself seated in your favourite chair, close your eyes and take three deep breaths.

- With each breath, breathe in through the nose and out through the mouth, taking each breath a little deeper.

- Each breath will have you sinking a little further and further into your chair as the mind frees itself from the day and the body begins to relax recognising what is to come.

- In your mind's eye imagine a door standing before you. Take a moment to reflect and notice how this door looks to you. Is it wood, intricately carved and beautiful to look at or is there something entirely unique about your door?

- As you stand before this door notice how you feel and any hesitation that you may feel. Acknowledge this and then proceed to open the door.

- Standing through the doorway is beautiful old Oak tree beckoning to you to come forth. As you bound up to it, you are taking in all of its glory, its sense of history and its unique beauty. How blessed you feel to be served by this glorious tree.

- Standing beneath the tree, in line with its tall trunk seek the wisdom and knowledge this tree holds for you by soaking up the energy of this majestic being.

- Take a moment to notice the presence of any other beings that may be joining you. It is all meaningful.

- Feel the energy and the presence of the tree. Rejoice in how it feels and be aware of any moment you may feel unbalanced. At those times, ask the tree to reveal to you what is needed to create balance and harmony here.

- Take as long as you feel is necessary here with your Oak tree and when you feel the energy begin to dissipate, gently bring your awareness back to your body by wriggling your finger and toes. In your own time, opening your eyes.

- Celebrate the magic and wisdom of all that you have received by making notes in your journal and giving back all that you have received by showing nature a little love today. Water a plant, collect some rubbish from the local park or even plant a tree in honour of the gift you have received today.

ALLOWING

Within the realms of creativity lies a clear and present process. It is one of create, accept and allow. As we come to this stage of Allowing, you begin to see the first signs of your goal, your heart's desire become a physical reality for you. All of your hardwork, the goal setting, the taking action, the often painful road of acceptance has lead you here.

It is in the space of allowing that your awareness needs to remain high. Be aware of how the universe is whispering to you at all times. Feel your way through each sign and indicator of the way forward and where relevant ensure you are open and accepting of how the Universe needs to deliver your wish. Keep yourself free of expectation and needing the outcomes to be a certain way.

Only the other day I was working with a Soul Purpose client whose goal is to have a job that feeds her soul, her passion and allows her to enjoy life. During her session her Soul communicated to me that there was a Soul Agreement associated with one of her other lives for her to travel to third world countries and give back by carrying out humanitarian work for the poor and starving. While this resonated with Amy and she did have a long term goal to do this, Amy was still focused on how to find the right corporate job that would feed her soul. I felt strongly that no office job would do this for her, that in fact Amy needed to focus on this overseas trip for its purpose of humanitarism and once this occurred, she would find the trip life changing. Amy would then be able to see how life could be different and more importantly, find the work that did feed her Soul.

Therefore acting on this Soul urge was important and failing to do so would see Amy with a life long sense of restlessness and continuing to try and make it all "fit" with how she thought life should be. Instead of allowing the Soul and its sense of connection to the Universe to whisper to her how it incredible it can be.

When we do let go of control in this way, freeing ourselves from expectation and let the Soul with its infinite wisdom guide us through intuition then magic truly begins to touch your life.

Part Three

Soul Centered Living

$\mathcal{T}$oday I woke to the presence of the Indian Goddess Durga. I recognised this Goddess from the image I received clairvoyantly of her many arms and being this is not a usual energy for me to connect with I certainly did need to do a little research to obtain some knowledge on what she represents.

Known as the Mother Goddess of the Universe, Durga is believed to be the power behind creation, preservation and destruction within the world. Hindus believe she protects her devotees from evil while removing their anguish and miseries.

Being this was a highly unusual visit for me, I knew to be mindful and to take some time to honour this visit with listening and writing what it was what she wanted to share with me. As I wrote I discovered that Goddess Durga wanted to open Part 3 of the book, so the following are her words as they came to me for you.

"We feed the Ego with our will. Our will can so easily override what the Soul knows unless we approach life with a sense of reverence. Giving it a mindfulness approach, one foot in front of the other at our own pace – not the pace that society tries to deem from us. It is only then that life begins to transform to the intentions of the Soul. Through listening in every moment of every day.

Your author initially intended to put pen to paper around the subject of relationship at the beginning of this section, then the intention shifted to discussing careers first. While all along, the intention of the Spirit was to bring it back to humbleness, to understand that underlying all of your creative efforts is the Soul, through which you build life upon. And to hear what the Soul wants, all you need do is listen. Just as your author has given some mindfulness to the thoughts of humbleness she awoke with today. Those thoughts, along with her listening and honouring grew into what you read before you. And I honour her and you today with a message of understanding, so the light and graciousness within you may shine forth."

Having this unfold in this way as I begin Part three of the book for you, really reflects how life can be when living from the Soul. We begin all of our creative endeavours with an idea or goal of what we wish to achieve in mind, which are largely derived from our sense of will. Yet underlying all of this, is the Souls intention and its path of evolution.

Your greatest successes, your happiness, your peace and sense of fulfillment, and a life filled with JOY will come when you combine your will with listening to the Soul which will have you walking hand in hand with your Spiritual destiny.

One question remains though – how do you apply these principals to the practical everyday aspects of living in today's world. A world where largely our careers, relationships and having enough money is important to us. This section is intended to give you those practical and simple everyday solutions and greater understandings to bring yourself more into vibrational alignment with what your Soul intends for you with these aspects of your life, knowing of course that your Soul has all the answers and what lies within your Soul ultimately aligns within the desires of your heart too.

Career Choices

When we map our lives and chart the course for success, our careers and what we do to earn a living are often of significant importance. Many of us have a Soul purpose intimately entwined with what we do in our area of work and more and more there is a collective shift occurring which has people making their career choices more firmly based on what they are passionate about, what they love to do and leaving behind the focus of just satisfying the obligations of providing as previous generations lived.

Doing this successfully does have an art to it and it begins by listening to the Soul's voice and the thoughts and subtle urges it has inspired you with throughout the years. Those thoughts of 'Gee, I'd really like to......" Insert whatever relevant thought has persisted for you over time, whether it is you wanting to write a book, work with animals, become a teacher or a nurse or even create a business around what is now a hobby for you, all of these thoughts are the Soul's way of letting you know what it wants, its desires and what is truly right for you.

Now before you jump into those thoughts of "Yeah, that's well and good but I do need to earn a living because I have rent or a mortgage to pay and put food on the table", stay with me just a little longer with this.

One of the mistakes we humans make is categorising the idea and projecting to what we think is the final outcome. Then getting overwhelmed because we cannot see how to get from point A to point B. Let's take the idea of creating a business around your hobby and let's pretend that your dream is to teach mothers and daughters how to cook and decorate wedding cakes for their special day. I met a lady once who had always wanted to do this.

It is ok for you not to know how to go about making this happen and you certainly do not need to be giving away any current job that is meeting your financial needs. Work towards transitioning from one way of life to another and know that all good things take time. Begin by researching what you need to know, whether it is business basics or even cake decorating if needed from our example. The important thing is to make the commitment within your heart and mind, then choosing to incorporate daily choices and actions that lead you to this goal. Doing this then sets the Universe in motion to support you, and the more action you take the more you will be carried along by synchronicity.

It is also important to keep your mind open to how the Universe wants to deliver your heart's desire. Just the other day, I met a lady who said she had always wanted to be a teacher but was definitely not in a position to make the change to return to study and create this lifestyle change. I pointed out to her that sometimes there is more than one way to satisfy want the Soul needs and it can be far simpler than you think. In this instance, I suggested she might like to volunteer teaching under priviledged children to read for example. Her response was that she used to teach children's bible study at church and found a lot of satisfaction in that. Perfect! Returning to dedicating some time to being of service in this way can have immense outcomes on how you feel. The Soul revels in the opportunity to be of service, to contribute and make a difference in this world in areas that are really important to you and often it does not need to be some grandious or complicated plan, just a couple of hours a week like this example can have your Soul at peace, knowing itself and projecting the gentle flowing energy of love and joy into other areas of your life.

Recognise where you may not be a current energetic vibrational match for your dream to come to fruition right now. Personally I am a prime example of this, where I have spent many years learning, growing and adjusting my vibration to match and align my Soul to be the successful author, speaker and medium that I aimed to be. Some of those adjustments meant gaining a thicker skin and believing in myself, just as much as it meant learning Mediumship, the Soul, internet marketing and publishing.

As you go through this process of alignment what is not right for you will reveal itself just as much as what is right, will. Trust your choices and know as long as you have kept your long term vision in your heart, every step is leading you closer and closer to achieving your dream.

EXERCISES

Practically co-creating a career path that is Soul inspired does begin with listening within as I have just explained, then next conscious awareness needs to become the focus to create successfully. That is taking conscious, concerted actions while also being ever mindful of when synchronicity presents in your life to progress you forward. To aide with the creative pathway while taking action, I recommend applying the principals outlined in the previous chapter – Your Creative Spirit.

You are manifesting your reality and giving the Soul a voice in deciding your career path. In doing so success will be forth coming, though it does take mindfulness and the power of the creative spirit to magnetise it and bring it all forth for you. Here are some daily Soul Conversations to help unlock the Soul's desire should you not know what you want to do or what career is best for you.

DAILY SOUL CONVERSATIONS:

"My Soul wants me to know that what I need to be right now for work is ……"

"My Soul says that my best and most fulfilling career choice is ……"

"My Souls say that the career totally aligned with the path of my Soul purpose is ……"

This Daily Soul Conversation will have you moving towards the career aligned with your Soul purpose each day. Remember, it is imperative to follow through on any action that is identified.

"Today, to move me closer to the career that is aligned with my Soul purpose I need to ……"

And this Daily Soul Conversation is designed for you should you already know what your Soul's career of choice is and you need the

Soul's assistance to achieve more success with it.

"Today, my Soul says that my heart, mind and soul are all in alignment with my Soul's purpose and to reveal what it is I need to do today to move me closer to achieving............ (insert specific career goal or aspiration), I need to ......"

One of the most powerful manifestation tools you can use is the Creative Intentions Soul Profile. More commonly used to manifest a new partner based on a list of characteristics, you can apply this tool to just about anything. A new house, the Soul clients you want to attract in your business or even the right publisher to publish your book, just as I did. Funny thing though, it turned out that I was the perfect match for my own Soul Publisher profile.

Manifesting work or a career is the ideal instance to use a Creative Intention Soul Job/Career profile. Essentially, by creating this profile you are effectively saying to the Universe "When you deliver my new job, please be aware that this list is what I need to align with my Soul and make my Soul sing, thank you." In fact, I would write this at the top of your list, as if you were writing a letter to the Universe.

Here are some guidelines to follow when compiling your list of creative intentions.

- Begin by taking your journal or a piece of paper.

- Over a quiet cup of coffee or tea take your time to write your list of intentions. It is important that this is done in solitude enabling you to extend beyond the mind, into the heart and soul.

- When compiling your list of intentions begin with writing down how you want the job to make you feel. For example:
  Happy.
  inSpired.

Enthusiastic.
Enable you to learn new things.
Enable you to help others.
Specifically work with children/animals/music/art or any hearts desire that is important to you.
Ability to make new friends.

- Once you've exhausted this, next continue your list by writing down characteristics you desire of your future employer. Here are a some suggestions:

    An employer who values their staff.
    Recognises and rewards effort and staff contribution.
    Compassionate to the work and home life balance.
    Exudes integrity and professionalism.

- Lastly, get specific with the day to day aspects of the job and having it meet your needs.

    Located close to home.
    A minimum weekly pay of ....

Working Hours or Days per week.

Once you have completed your letter to the Universe, sign it and date it. This all contributes to asserting your commitment and strengthening the Universe's ability to deliver.

As you move through the pathway of taking action to make your new job or career a reality, be sure to refer to your Creative Intention Job profile before you fully accept and commit to any new job offer or embarking on a new career path. You want to ensure your new job ticks all the boxes, that's for sure.

If it doesn't match and something is missing from your profile you will need to decide if you can compromise on it or if living without it will still have your Soul sing. If not, then don't be afraid to say no to this opportunity. By doing so you are letting the Universe know it was a good try, though a little fine tuning is still needed. Try to avoid falling into the trap of accepting anything that feels "less than" and doesn't really match your profile, doing this will see you creating more of that which is "less than" and not just in the area of your work life. It will filter through to your home and your personal life too. So fine tune how you co-create with the Universe by taking the time to acknowledge and honour any reservations or fears you may have. Use your journal and follow up with another letter to the Universe.

"Hi Universe, I'm just touching base to let you know how I feel about what has transpired recently and I need to reaffirm or adjust my needs………….(elaborate here) Thank you"

Manifesting a job or career that is aligned with your soul is really no different to manifesting anything else in this life. It is all energy and during the creative process you are essentially fine tuning the energetics to match your vibration with the vibration of the job.

The Soul's Purpose and its pre-birth intention does contribute to the overall outcomes should the circumstances of your Soul Purpose require a job or specific career to unfold your Soul Purpose. Not all Soul Purpose's do by the way. However, by simply listening to your Soul, its wants and desires as you are here, you are giving yourself the highest potential to live your Soul Purpose.

Aligning With Money

Money is the one thing we all find ourselves in conflict with from time to time. Be it, not having enough to help life flow a little easier or finding yourself caught up in a quarrel over money from a friend not repaying your loan and your gift of generosity, to family conflict over a loved ones last will and testament that requires legal action to come to a resolution. At one time or another we have all been presented with challenges regarding money and wealth. Why is this?

Money is our primary source of energy exchange and it is also largely how we as a society identify our value and worth. Not just for ourselves but for everything that exists in this world. If you look about you right now, in this moment everything you see has a dollar value attached to it. It is this currency that impacts your world everyday, from the cup of coffee you may have just purchased to the house you live in and what it says about your standing in society, to how much you earn for the job you do. Especially how much you earn for the job you do! Subconsciously, all of these currency exchanges equates to you placing a value on who you are without even thinking about it. Then most people will value themselves from a place of lack as they struggle with self worth issues.

In this moment my higher self intercedes.

"Money is the means through which your society values itself. It is seen as the metric gauge for what everything is worth, including

people. So the question begs then, what are you worth? Are you worth what society says you are or so much more?"

Especially if you happen to be in business for yourself and be a Soulpreneur like myself, are your services worth more than the current market trend?

With a lot of people trying to overcome financial challenge while harbouring a lack of self worth, it is only when you recognise the connection between the two, money and your self worth that healing can begin and you can truly effect change to your financial circumstances.

While I may focus this writing and explanations on the more common experience of not having enough money, the same truth lies in any challenge faced when you do have enough or plenty of wealth but for one reason or another, peace and JOY alludes you as you find yourself constantly trying to overcome challenges associated with your wealth. It all centers around the value you hold true for yourself as an individual and the value you equate others with.

Is it really necessary to see yourself through the eye of society's monetary metric system. No, certainly not! There is success and worth in much that you do that is not associated with money. We are just not conditioned to see it as worthy or as a measure of success. We are not taught that volunteering, humanitarism and being there for one another is a form of success. That helping another soul be abundant will see yourself be abundant in return, for what goes around comes around.

Again my higher self would like to interject here *"Teach your children this and life will be very different in the generations to come. Your planet largely operates from a place of lack causing disharmony and imbalance on many levels. And while there is movement to rectify this within the collective consciousness, it is not enough. Until such time as there is, people on your planet will continue to starve, harm will continue to others and animals will continue to suffer. Until awareness comes to see that the root of all this, which you think is rooted in money, is seen and understood to be a lack of valuing of the self and seeing yourself, the human race as the creation and light of God that you are, no real change can occur.*

What we can ask you do though, is be the change you want to see in the world*. See yourself for who you truly are. Value yourself, your integrity, your strength, your knowledge and go out into the world knowing you have a responsibility and contribution to make. In doing so, the plan of love and light will work out*. You will be raising awareness and helping others to see these truths, one Soul at a time."

Once again where money is concerned, keep in mind always that the amount of money showing up in your life is directly related to your sense of self worth and your ability to express this in the world around you. When faced with any challenges ask yourself this Soul Conversation and fill in the blank with the option that is more relevant for you:

"How can I value myself more in this situation so that...

1. I can receive more money.

2. This situation can resolve itself.

3. I can bring more humbleness to the wealth I already have.

Occasionally, people are born into this world with one of your Soul Agreements focused on money where it is part of your pre-birth plan and life circumstances designed to support your Soul Purpose. These agreements vary from achieving wealth, even winning the lottery, overcoming hardship to become financially independent, engaging in philanthropy, becoming a beggar on the other end of the scale and going without for a purpose. All of which are designed to assist your Soul's evolution.

It is also entirely possible to have no Soul Agreement arrangement assigned to money and wealth and therefore you have your total destiny where money is concerned entirely in your conscious creative hands. In this instance, it truly is what you make of it so get goal setting right now!

Or like me, you may have entered into this work taking on the responsibility of others and working towards balance for humanity. As I understand it, in this incarnation it is imperative for me and my Soul to be highly conscious of giving back when creating wealth. To help others create abundance, as I do and strive to help others be successful. This has been a natural component to the work I do and has grown the more aligned to the Divine my Soul has become. Over the years I have mentored and supported many developing mediums to forge forth in their new careers and even inSpirit Magazine and inSpirit Publishing has this supportive nature at the core of that we do. It is only now that I have come to fully appreciate this aspect of who I am and why it shows itself in my business and life as it does.

Inherently, I know I have this other life (past life) that concurrently exists alongside mine where part of my soul group is incarnated in a time where men rule the land by hoarding property, renting it to the less fortunate and being ferociously cruel when money is not forthcoming. I don't have a lot of detail about this life except I clairvoyantly see a man on horseback in a village environment and I sense his wrath and murderous cruelty. I also know that at one point my lack of money was associated in feeling guilt due to this situation and subconsciously not allowing myself to create wealth due to what was occurring with this other life. Going within and seeking answers to changing my financial situation brought about this understanding, that once I had worked through the limitations I held associated with this life, my Soul then needed me to know how there was a lot more to it. Having grown and accepted that wealth is completely agreeable to receive, I know that in giving back and helping support others as I do, I am not only transforming my own situation with money, I am also energetically contributing positively to this man's life and helping to bring some balance to all those being affected by him. I sense I am helping to raise his awareness in some way as I raise my own around money and while I may never know or be able to fully appreciate the difference I am making, I trust in knowing we are all connected in Oneness where we are all connected to everyone and everything throughout all time and space where our Soul's connections can influence where we are at and the lives we live and beyond.

PROCESS OF ALIGNMENT

The challenges you face now, in this life incarnation are all overcome by aligning your vibration more closely with what it is you desire within the boundaries of any Soul agreement that may exist.

How do you know a Soul agreement exists for you regarding money?

- You feel it in your heart.

- You have great strength where money is concerned.

- It is a theme that runs throughout all of your life, from childhood and continues into adulthood. The circumstances may change somewhat, though it remains a focus and a concern with regular challenges.

If you are resonating with this then it is safe to say you have a Soul agreement involving money and you can uncover more specifics about your agreement by setting the intention, asking your Soul to reveal the agreement to you and then allowing the universe to whisper to you and follow your intuition where this is concerned.

Once you have identified whether a Soul agreement exists for you regarding money, you are then able to bring about healing to the situation if needed or you are free to create in this lifetime as you choose. Doing this is far simplier than people would have you believe though it does take action, commitment and belief.

Set your goals high, though one thing I would recommend when creating soul centered goals is to not set out creating money for the sake of wanting money or to try and rectify a lack of it. This invariably will be tough to achieve as essentially you are creating from a negative energy space. When living from your Soul, which is aligned with the Divine, money, energy and success will flow as a result of the energy you are putting into this world. What is it you are doing to earn money? Or attract money? Is it flowing from your heart and soul or from your ego self and largely bound by obligation, which will then be derived in limitation and therefore limit how much money will flow your way.

Break free from those boundaries with thinking outside the box and these fives principals to align with the flow of money.

1. Align Your Heart's Desire

Ensure your hearts desire is aligned with your passion and what makes your Soul sing. Remember this is the foundation from which you create, so ask yourself are you creating your life experience from a base which makes the soul Joyful, or are you stuck in obligation. Recognising this is the first step to change.

2. Visions, Goals, Affirmations and Daily Choices

Create your visions, goals, affirmations and daily choices supporting your hearts desire. Avoid creating them to 'fix a problem' and out of the energy of lack. The sponsoring energy beyond the problem is usually centered in lack and negativity, which will only create more of the same.

For example, instead of creating a goal where you see your bank accounts full or $30,000 in the next six months, try focussing your goals on doing what you love as opposed to what you want to get out of it.

One of my daily choices is to "Make money from doing what I love to do, each and every day building the freedom to do all that I want to do easily and effortlessly."

Focusing your efforts on the doing and being in the energy of your passion and hearts desire, is not only the ideal energy to create your life experience with, you'll be happy while your doing it too.

3. Accept that it is Ok to be Spiritual and Wealthy.

Being spiritual and wealthy are not mutually exclusive, in fact financial freedom allows you to do more, give more and therefore make an even bigger difference in this world that perhaps without money you wouldn't be able to do.

I know for me personally, there was a time when using the word wealthy, associated with me was uncomfortable. Thinking about even going into a Louis Vuitton shop would cause some anxiousness and doubt. Not that I actually even like Louis Vuitton! The feeling of being 'less than' would come up at any time when I was associated with wealth in some form. It was in getting to know who, I am in Oneness that allowed me to see this and affirm to Spirit that I love and accept myself for wanting to be wealthy. Because I know in being so, I can do more and this invariably does flow to others.

Be aware that aligning with thoughts or beliefs that using your Spiritual gifts need to shared freely because they are God given will keep your flow of money very limited. These beliefs feed your attraction point and in my experience, people who align with this set of beliefs usually also have an underlying lack of self belief. So if this speaks to you, if this pushes your button in any way delve a little deeper within and ask to be shown your truth.

All of us are born with unique talents and gifts, its what makes you, you. We are meant to be sharing them with the world, they are directly associated with your Soul Purpose. Whether it is the talent of inSpiration to create Apple products and lead the world forward through technology or being psychic and communicating with Spirit, we are all meant to receive in return. It is the way the law of creativity works. Our world uses money as its form of energy exchange, it is widely recognised in the western world as acknowledgement for goods and services rendered. So in giving, all you are asking for is the commonly recognised form of receiving in the exchange. All very normal and commonplace.

Accepting this leads to a greater sense of freedom and therefore allows the flow of creative energy to find you.

4. Allowing the Flow

Be aware - look for the inSpirations, intuitive impulses and synchronicities leading you forward to achieve what you've set your heart, soul and mind to.

Keep the focus of your daily choices to help create the flow. And if you encounter feeling stuck or blocked, revisit your daily choices to see where you've lost focus.

As you feel the flow and begin to receive, be mindful of giving to others in return. Being generous takes gratitude to a whole new level and for you keeps the energy flowing beautifully like a river. If you haven't yet reached the heights of wealth your looking for, it doesn't need to cost you money to give in this way. One of my favourite 'pay it forward' ideas is to use the FREE coffee I receive on my loyalty card and ask the barista to give it to the next person who comes in behind me. They don't need to know who its from, but I do enjoy watching their reaction, if I happen to taking the time to enjoy a sit down with my coffee.

5. enJOY as you recognize that JOY is the reward.

Soul Relationships

The last few days I have been pondering how to begin this chapter and just like in life, Spirit has responded in a way that infuses itself and demonstrates what living with inspiration is really like.

Yesterday, I felt drawn to pull a card from my friend psychic medium John Holland's new oracle deck Spirit Messages. The card that presented was the Relationship card. Of course! And while at the time I didn't know why I needed to draw a card, it quickly became apparent that Spirit was guiding the commencement of this chapter and what was to be discussed.

The card reads *"Relationships are just mirror images of your own life – how you feel and treat yourself, as well as how you react and respond to different situations and people around you. Be aware that every relationship is an opportunity for soul growth."©*

It seems to me that this short phrase epitomises what our relationship are all about. From global relationships between countries, right down to the relationship we have with one another, our pets and even the stranger you encounter during your day.

Walking unaware that the Divine Spirit is part of your makeup leaves you at the mercy of others and in a place of reacting to them and life, targeting ill will as the Ego self works hard at needing to protect and defend you in every situation. This is why we see war on a global scale and it is also why certain relationships or life in general feels like you are waging a war, constantly in the grind of fighting battle after battle.

When you begin to disarm yourself by feeling the presence of Spirit in your heart, magic begins to occur. You start to preclude yourself from people, environments and situations that no longer feel good and no longer align with your new vibration of love. In every group of people, I have ever taught or coached over the years, there is always someone who needs to ask about facing the challenge of losing friends and whether this is normal. Yes, it most certainly is and can be expected many times throughout your journey, should personal growth be a commitment you make to yourself.

Each time you grow into a new understanding, you are changing who you are, even if just a little. This means you develop new needs, new interests and are now attracting with a new vibration. The end result then sees people who no longer are a vibrational match leave your life and new people who do venture in. The challenge begins when either party resist and hold on, instead of accepting the soul energy and letting go, that the relationship ends painfully usually by imploding upon itself. Of course, you can learn from this but please do keep in mind not all such relationships need to end negatively. The key to working towards a positive ending when one of your relationships is in the process of separation is to bring the energy of awareness and compassion to it. Use the power of prayer and create a soul conversation to use that will help you reveal what is needed for you to move forward with love.

All relationships that are soul connected are derived from a soul agreement. These relationships, we commonly call Soul Mate relationships and they consist of the good, the bad and the ugly.

In this moment I hear *"Allow us to explain"* as my higher self seeks to connect with you.

"You see, all relationships allow you the opportunity to see yourself in them, as if looking in the mirror. It is in the interactions with others that you are reflected back to yourself. So what is it you want to know about yourself?"

Do you want to know how well you receive love? The answer lies in how other people treat you. Is there a distinct lack of love and appreciation towards you or are you enveloped in it everyday. Do you want to know how abundantly wealthy you are? Then look around at the people in your life. How well do they respond to money? Is it flowing for them or are they constantly struggling?

Breaking it down and seeing our relationships in this way is extremely powerful as it then allows you to respond with greater awareness to any given situation. For years my own marriage felt like a daily battle ground. One, where I was constantly in need of fighting back to defend myself in an effort to try and resist being treated disrespectfully. Only this wasn't the answer. Yes, I was asserting boundaries and not accepting the lack of respect, ultimately though it was a battle of wills. Until, I started to accept that I didn't need my husband's acceptance, approval or love in the way I expected it, and I came into loving and accepting myself independent of others. This then enabled me to take more of my own Ego out of the interactions and I could see my way to responding in a much smarter and heartfelt way. Being more selective about which battles I chose to fight and using words that still address the situation, but leave the other person thinking more about their intentions. And all of this happens naturally with a gentler flow of ease and grace for me.

Once you clear your own Ego self from getting in the way, you are then able to see the truth of your relationships. You can more clearly see the purpose of the relationship, its outcome and what if anything you can do to hold on to or let go of should you choose to.

Each of us have at least one if not more relationship Soul Agreements be it with our parents, siblings, children or even friends. In fact, the most common Soul Purpose is derived from a relationship that has a specific intention of soul evolution for all involved. All of these Soul Agreements being created before life as part of the map of your pre-birth plan where all parties have agreed to come together in life to support, nurture and work together to achieve the evolution of the soul for one or both parties.

If I look at the major relationships in my life that have all contributed exponentially to my soul growth and evolution, my mother, my brother and my husband have all provided experiences at different stages of life that have been needed to reach where I am today. Even now, I am keenly aware that my husband and I have come together in this lifetime to make amends from another lifetime, as he supports me in living out of my Soul Purpose, he in turn is living out his Soul Purpose as well.

Even in death, a Soul Agreement can still be equally implemented and lived across the worlds. Firstly, my brother Allen's death provided the spiritual awakening I needed to really connect with the path that has lead me to my Soul Purpose, however even now he is still an important part of living it out and the work I am here to do. On occasion I feel him supporting me, and when I need a little extra guidance he often makes himself known through friends or other mediums letting me know he is fully aware, still part of the team and helping where it is needed. Just the other day, I had tipped my hat in the ring to audition for an upcoming TV pilot for a show based on Mediumship. I wasn't feeling very connected to the project so I wasn't really that surprised when my application was declined citing a conflict of interest over our publishing businesses. The next day, I received a sign from Allen letting me know all is as it needs to be when the Medium behind this TV pilot was posting Facebook the need to find who a Spirit named Allen belonged to. Once confirmed, I knew Allen was holding my hand and guiding things as always.

Not all relationships you encounter, however are created in the form a Soul Agreement. Many people you connect with throughout your life are certainly there to play a role and fulfill a need, however the creative energy they are derived from which magnetizes it into existence can come from two completely different places.

One is centered in the Divine Spirit connection, its depths and is sparked into existence at the time of your pre-birth plan, which is the Soul Agreement relationship we have been discussing. These relationships are part of your destiny and will always find a way into your life. The other is simply the law of attraction playing out where you attract people to you based on the vibration of your soul and your energetic makeup. Commonly, these relationships are often attracted to placate and supply a need within the Ego self such as the synchronicity of two souls meeting to move one of them forward in life or business, or the simple art of being at one with another soul in friendship, partnership or family.

I was talking with Alana recently when her Soul revealed to me that her first marriage which was a long and abusive marriage, need not have occurred. There was no Soul Agreement in place calling for it to be destined, yet Alana had magnetised this relationship with her current set of beliefs, thoughts and sense of self worth she held for herself at the time. I'm not saying all abusive relationships are created in this way, for if there is one thing I know about understanding how the Soul operates, it is that there is no rule of thumb. Each and every relationship has it's own unique reason for being and it is not until you become intimate in knowing your own Soul self that those reasons can be revealed to you.

THE RELATIONSHIP MAP EXERCISE

Let's take some time to look a little closely at all the significant relationships in your life. This process will reveal a little insight into the purpose of each relationship and whether or not it is derived from a Soul Agreement.

1. Take a piece of paper or your journal and draw a series of circles just like the diagram on the next page

2. Within each circle write the name of those who are close to you, people who have meant a lot to you and who you hold close to your heart. Also include those you feel who have had a big influence in your life but may not be part of your life now.

3. Allow each name to come forward into your mind on it's own and place it in the appropriate circle. As you do, pay close attention to your intuition and any other thoughts that arise around the relationship.

SOUL RELATIONSHIP MAP

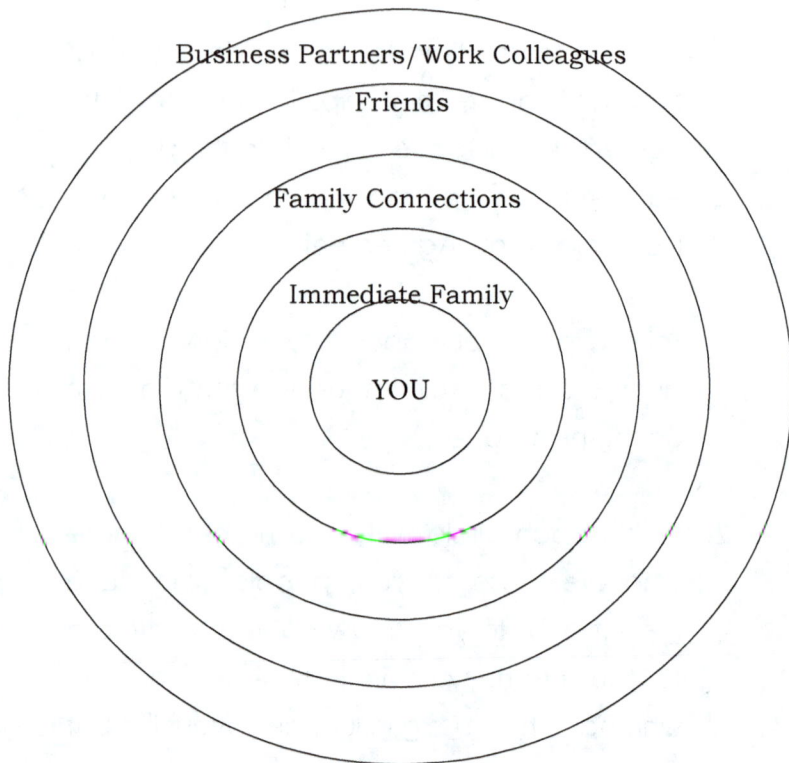

Immediate Family:

partners, children, siblings and parents.

Family Connections:

extended family, cousins, aunts, uncles and grandparents.

Write it all in your journal and lastly ask this Soul Conversation

"Is my relationship with …………..(insert a name) created with a Soul Agreement between us?"

4. You will feel the answer within your being. It will have its own energy prompting your intuition. Should it feel empty and a 'nothingness' exists with the thoughts, this is answering with a 'No' to your Soul Conversation.

5. Repeat steps 3 and 4 until you feel you have exhausted all the inSpiration and the relationship in your life.

Your Soul Purpose Revealed

Joy is the Reward

Firstly, it is important for you to know it is within you to discover your Soul Purpose whether you live with the knowing you are the Divine Spirit or not. Living with the knowing that you are a spark of the Divine Spirit, that your life is an expression of God has one simple reward – JOY.

Life is full of JOYous moments as you discover who you truly are and live each moment of the day feeling the energy that pervades all of life. Wonderment becomes your friend as you constantly find yourself in amazement at each of the little miracles life has to offer you and the rewards do not stop there.

Walking the path of love and inspiration fulfills many of your heart desires and it will also see the actualisation of your Soul's Purpose – without question and without the need to try to hard. Fulfilling your Soul's Intention and aligning with your pre-birth plan is a matter of course and is the end result, when you live each day listening to the inner stirrings of the Soul. Your Destiny's Plan will work out as it was originally intended.

Remember, you have designed a life that inexplicably supports the original intention your Soul has for this lifetime. From the country you were born in, your parents and family dynamics to the major life experiences that signpost your journey. All of this is part of your pre-birth plan and are really not dependant on whether you live with the knowing that you are a spark of the Divine or not.

In my work I come across so many people who are looking to discover their Soul Purpose, yet do not realise they are already living it. We have such grand illusions about what the Soul's Purpose is. We think or want our Soul Purpose to be special, for it to change our lives, to change the lives of others, to change the world and by doing so we want to live a life that is abundant, free and enriching.

For some of you, living your Soul Purpose is all of this and more. For many of you though, your Soul Purpose is already woven through the life you are already living. It is in the relationships you have loved and lost, and how you all help one another evolve. It is in the love you have for animals and the caring you give to one of God's creatures. It is in the being there for a friend in their time of need and giving them love, that is Spirit's way and it is the work you have chosen to do because it makes your heart sing and you feel it makes a difference.

When you break it down, it is the everyday choices you make that align you to your Soul Purpose or not. Intuitive based choices, choices from the heart will do this. Those choices you know, you can't live without and are really no choice at all because you can't see yourself doing anything else. And we have all made plenty of those kind of choices.

Choices that are based in obligation, expectation, pleasing others and the will of the self to placate your unconscious behaviours of the Ego will and can lead you away from your Divine Self and your Soul Purpose. The path of your spiritual destiny will try to right itself in time through those 'wake up' moments that occur in life, but knowing yourself as the Divine being of Love that you are, is and always will be a conscious choice.

One choice that you make each day that can make a radical difference to how you experience life. The difference between seeing a weed or a flower, the storm or not a cloud in sight and the difference between a JOYous, Love filled experience to that of a life that never quite satisfies, that lacks in love and appreciation, always filled with so called drama and never has you reaching the heights of success and abundance you are truly capable of.

As I was preparing to end the book with this chapter, Spirit gave me a dream that exemplifies that living your Soul Purpose does not automatically equate to peace and happiness. In the dream, I was meeting Country music star Keith Urban and if you know me or have been following my work, you will know how momentous this would be for me. Anyway, I took the opportunity to tell Keith how inSpirational he has been for me having followed his journey over the last twenty years. From humble beginnings in Australia, through drugs and alcohol addiction all the while staying true to his dream and Soul Purpose. He totally deserves his success and the life he now lives with wife, actress Nicole Kidman. As I said all of this to Keith and thanked him for being an inspiration, Nicole says to me "Keith doesn't believe all of that", and it triggered him into a spiral of depression that saw him retreat to spending days in bed. I woke up as I was making moves to go and help.

I don't for one minute think this is a true representation of Keith Urban, in fact I'm confident in my thinking that Keith does now believe in himself and has plenty of love and faith in himself and this is why he now exudes what it means to live your Soul Purpose in a way that is aligned with Love.

Spirit's intention in offering me this dream was to remind you that you can be living your Soul Purpose and achieving some success with it, like Keith did with his first few albums before he met Nicole, though unless you combine it with aligning with love and the Spirit of the Divine, peace and happiness will still allude you.

It is only when you come into this alignment of Love and inSpiration that the success of living your Soul Purpose can reach heights far beyond your expectations and the JOY can only be experienced to truly know how it feels.

Acknowledgements

Writing a book for me becomes a living experience as Spirit guides me to people, experiences and connections that are required for me to be able to fill the pages of any book I write. Whether it is personal growth and new learning I needed or the support one needs when bringing a book to life everyone that is mentioned here in the acknowledgements needs my heartfelt thanks and gratitude. You have all played a role in creating Wisdom of the Soul however small, yet in doing so by touching my life you have helped me bring this wisdom into the world to help others. Thankyou.

Kim Forrester, thank you for your friendship and more importantly intuiting that the information I was psychically receiving was for the purpose of a new book. Who knows how long it would have taken me to get it!

Nicolle Poll, you are a source of inspiration, my publishing right hand and a dear friend I cherish. Thank you so much for your friendship, editing my books, your guidance and help. I appreciate and love you.

William Whitecloud that weekend of experiencing your Genius at work truly changed my life and who I am, all of which certainly made creating Wisdom of the Soul possible. Thank you. I am so grateful for your work and pray that you continue to reach millions of people so you may change each of their lives in similar ways.

Jodie Smart and Christine Rizk, your friendship and presence in my life over the last couple of years certainly made the days amongst my soft place to land much sweeter. Thank you.

My NFF's, I love each and everyone of you. You help me laugh, enjoy life and feel safe in the knowing that some friendships are supportive, fun, sharing and quite simply about being who we are. Who's up for an Orange Mocha Frappacino at coffee next week?

And lastly to my family, Rod, Nathan and Jessica, thank you for the JOY you bring to my life each and everyday. I love you deeply and pray with all my heart that one day soon, you may take the Wisdom of the Soul principals to heart and create the life I deeply desire for you.

About the Author

Kerrie Wearing is a soul coach, a medium and author of A New Kind of Normal: Unlock the Medium Within. Kerrie is passionate about helping people to live their Soul Purpose knowing they are One with Spirit and coaching Mediumship practitioners to achieve high levels of integrity, professionalism and accuracy of Mediumship through strong foundations with Spirit.

She is also founder and managing director of inSpirit Magazine and Publishing. A high quality magazine offering Spiritual solutions for Soul centred living. With over 15 years of professional experience, Kerrie is highly regarded within the international spiritual community.

Kerrie lives in Sydney, Australia with her husband, two young adult children, two dogs and lives a not so secret life as a Country Music fan.

Kerrie is also the author of *A New Kind of Normal: Unlock the Medium Within* and the *Daily Soul Conversation inSight* cards.

To connect with Kerrie please visit
Website: www.kerriewearing.com
Facebook: www.facebook.com/kerriewearingmedium
Twitter: www.twitter.com/kerriewearing

www.ingramcontent.com/pod-product-compliance
Lightning Source LLC
Chambersburg PA
CBHW071908290426
44110CB00013B/1326